Holding On For Dear Life: What My Fatal Diagnosis Taught Me About Living

Holding On For Dear Life: What My Fatal Diagnosis Taught Me About Living

Liz DeVivo

ISBN-13: 9780692755129
ISBN-10: 0692755128

To all those that came before and all those who will come after.

Table of Contents

Preface

My initial intent for this book was to explore the idea of chronic illness and early death.

However, people have told me-- repeatedly-- that if anything, my story has given them the much-needed perspective to realize what things are-- and aren't-- so bad in their lives.

Now, more than ever, people need to prioritize what is truly important, what is less important, and what is not important at all. My experiences clearly define what ultimately is important for me today. My hope is that through my journey, people will look beyond their immediate needs, redefine their priorities, and see what truly matters in life.

Growing up in the wake of the Baby Boomers, there was never a shortage of information, advice, or how-to expertise for any milestone in my life.

I grew up with books that taught me how to pick a career, how to live my life, how to love, how to marry, how to have a healthy pregnancy, how raise a baby, child, teenager... you get the picture.

In 2000, when at the age of 33, I was told I had incurable and terminal illness. I was given a life expectancy of 2--5 years. My natural response was not to walk, but to run to the self-help section of the bookstore. At the bookstore I searched desperately for information on this latest, and very unwelcome, stage of my life.

I found books that talked about death and dying, other books on how to care for the dying, and stories of grief and loss from the perspective of the ones left behind. There was not a whole lot on how to live despite being told you were dying, or anything about the grief and loss the *dying* person experiences.

I felt betrayed by the Boomers. How could an entire generation let me down? Then I realized that I had beaten most Boomers to this area of concern. Lucky me.

I wanted a book that would help me not only with all the concrete end-of-life choices that I needed to make (this type of book already existed), but also with additional emotional information-- something that might help me peacefully come to terms with the end of my life. Better yet, what I really wanted was a book that would help me survive regardless what the medical personnel and literature said.

In essence, I was looking for a book entitled "How to Live a Happy Life Despite Being Told You Are Dying", or even better yet, "How to **Survive** and Live a Happy Life Despite Being Told That You Are Dying". What I wanted was hope.

But alas, I could not find either title.

Which is what lead me to this endeavor.

For better and for worse, I know first-hand the many complicated components (physical, psychological, emotional, and financial) of being ill-- and, more importantly, staying well. I understand the everyday intricacies of *navigating* a catastrophic illness, and the toll it takes--not only on the diagnosed individual, but on the family/caregivers as well. My professional training as a therapist/ social worker, coupled with my horrific disease(s), gave me insight and taught me many lessons that make for interesting, thoughtful and sometimes comical reading.

My advice is barely that rather, it is more a sharing of my life experiences and difficulties, in the hope of validating other peoples' experiences. Dying and end-of-life issues are often ignored and shunned in our culture, mostly because of the discomfort it creates. For the most part, people just twitch and change the subject.

Even further, talking about death is only tolerated when you are talking of living the best life you can. Our culture does not embrace this stage of life as part of the life cycle; although fortunately, the times, they are a-changing.

I don't pretend to know it all, or even a lot for that matter. I know I beat the odds. What follows is my story--and yes, some advice. My Story, as told thru my online web journal, what we now call a blog. When started in 2001, 18 months into my illness, this journal was just a means to an end, a way to communicate broadly with family and friends. A website very much like caringbridge.org now operates. Initially, this was nothing more than a simple website set up by friends to help fundraise for my transplant. Over time it evolved and took on a life of its own.

Now, this book is part journal, part practical and concrete advice on negotiating "the system", and part emotional advice for the soul. I have also included thoughts for health care professionals when dealing with patients in general, and chronically ill patients in particular.

I thought that by sharing some of my experience I could provide a sense of validation for people going through similar difficulties. But please remember this as you read: the time frame is early in the 2000s, and thankfully much has changed in medical practice, treatment and scientific research. What was true for me 10 years ago may no longer hold true now. I realize the treatments and medications I might speak about may no longer be standard protocol; please try not to get caught up in this. What matters is that I am still here to tell the tale. I ask the readers, especially those with similar circumstances, to be understanding and accepting of this fact.

Who I was before my illness.

⁓

I was 33, married and living in Vestal, New York, home of Binghamton University, when I was told I was terminally ill. My children, Emma and Luci, were 4 and 7.

I remember thinking at the time, not a little bitterly, that Jesus was 33 when he died, and look at all he accomplished in his life. I looked at myself and asked, *what have you accomplished with yours?* I asked myself that question not because I was religious (because at that time I was not), but because I had gone to Catholic school for 12 years, and it was my frame of reference.

My illness happened at a time in my life when I thought I was doing all the things I should be doing. I was a mother of a toddler and kindergartner, and I was finishing my masters' degrees, because it's what I thought I should be doing. I graduated in May 1999 and my husband, Scott, and I bought a house and moved into it in July 1999. My oldest daughter Luci, was transitioning to a new school for first grade, it was an exciting time for all of us except for my little Emma who stated "I don't want move to a new house; I like my old toys at the old house". She became a bit more excited when we explained to her that the old toys could come to the new house.

All the excitement of a new home and career came to a screeching halt a mere nine months later when I became ill. My to-do list which previously listed innocuous chores like "paint the bedroom" and "buy new sofa", was thrown away and replaced by a much more dismal list. My list included wills, directives, and goodbye letters to my family. Talk about not wanting to do your "chores".

I wrote my husband a goodbye letter, what I thought would be his last love letter from me.

Dearest Scott,

First of all, I want to thank you for the many years of laughter you have given me. You know of course that this is the reason I married you....only you could make me laugh like you do. I hope we have many years left together, but I am not sure that is going to happen.

We had so many plans and things left to do, so much fun yet to be had....I feel robbed.

It isn't fair.

Anyway, I am sure there is more for us - even if it's not in this lifetime, I am sure of that!

I am sorry for all the torture I have brought upon you, us and our family. I wish you peace, love and happiness too (I know these are hard to come by these days).

I wish I could tell you to never remarry, since you see I'll be jealous even from the grave - but I can't say that. I hope you do find love, just remember to give yourself some time. Please don't introduce the girls to any girlfriends, or dates unless you are absolutely positive you want them to be part of your family's life.

Be patient and kind with our children and always remember they are girls, a different breed than what you are used to. I am sure they will teach you a lot. I think you are a wonderful parent. The girls are lucky to have you. You are a great Dad.

I was lucky to have you.

All my love,

Liz

I knew that when I had my children I wanted to be with them as much as possible. Like many families, we couldn't afford for me to stay home full time, so for us that meant working part time. One of the reasons I went to graduate school was to get the certification I needed in order to get into a school system as a social worker. Eventually, like many mothers, I thought it would be ideal to be able keep the same schedule as my children--again, because it was what I thought I should be doing.

Up until graduate school, I had worked as an intensive case manager helping to keep children out of foster care whenever possible. It was a difficult, stressful, but rewarding job that required a great deal of flexibility and being on call, at times 24/7. I knew it was not a family-friendly job, and it was with that knowledge that I returned to school. My goal was to get in sync with my girls.

The first illness, scleroderma, I had known about for a few years, since the birth of my second daughter. The symptoms began during my pregnancy. It was 1996, I was 30 years old and pregnant when I had the first symptom. Reynaud's syndrome, (when your hands and feet turn different shades of red white or blue--not because you're patriotic, but because of circulation problems), and an elevated ANA level (elevated anti-nuclear antibodies usually indicate some type of auto-immune disease, like lupus).

The doctors reassured me that it wasn't uncommon to have these symptoms during pregnancy and that they'd likely go away after I had my baby.

But, the ANA level stayed high and the Reynaud's did not go away. At first they called it Mixed Connective Tissue Disease. Three years later, after having some additional symptoms and MANY, MANY more tests, they were finally able to identify it as Scleroderma.

Scleroderma literally means *hardening of the skin*, and it is an autoimmune disease. Its most simplistic explanation is when your body overproduces collagen. It can over-produce collagen on the outside of your body, on your skin, making it thick and hard; or it can happen internally to your organs, hardening your kidneys, lungs or heart.

When I was first diagnosed, my hands and face were changing, therefore I was told I had the 'outside' kind what was then called CREST (an acronym for its 5 main features). I was relieved to know it was considered the lesser-evil of the two options. In February 2000, the doctors ran all kinds of tests on my organs to determine the extent of the scleroderma, and to create a baseline (swallowing tests, pulmonary functions tests, and cardiac tests). Thankfully, they found no internal manifestations

That is until May of 2000, a mere three months later.

I distinctly remember that weekend, because I was content to count massive amounts of change out of the change jar with my children on the living room floor, only because it didn't require ANY physical movement out of me. Little did I know that this inertia would soon become a way of life for me and that in a little over a year I would be listed and waiting desperately for an organ transplant.

December 2001

⟶

Tuesday, December 11, 2001

I am not a writer. Never have been. I don't write literature, great novels or even essays for that matter. I wrote my way through my Bachelor's because I had to, then I wrote through my Masters and then my second Masters. So why am I writing this?

I am ill. I am waiting for a lifesaving transplant. I have no choice. If I had a choice I would be sharing this story with everybody in person. I would tell my story somehow through my mouth, which was at one time, (before the disease) very large and loud. Now talking leaves me breathless and my mouth has literally shrunk. So I will attempt to tell a story by writing it. The only modality left to me at this time.

I hope I can do myself some justice. So think of it as storytelling- in written form
-- Liz

Thursday, December 13, 2001

So I guess I need to speak a little about my illness(es). I'm not sure how it all happened, but I'll share what I can to the best of my ability.

In May of 2000 I started feeling out of breath-- more so than usual. Daily activities, simple ones like running errands and climbing stairs were leaving me breathless and tired. I had always kind of chalked it up to lack of exercise.

I had been diagnosed with scleroderma a few years earlier. Scleroderma is a disease of the body's connective tissue, where one's immune system mistakenly attacks and destroys healthy tissue. But for having what is considered to be a chronic disease, my symptoms were mild, and I didn't think of it very often. Rather than blame these new bouts of shortness of breath on either an existing condition or

5

a new one, I instead blamed myself for being lazy—despite having a 4- and 7-year old, and recently completing two master's degrees.

I had recently in effort to combat my laziness committed myself to an exercise class, and a ballet class. I could barely get through either class, without having to stop to catch my breath, by strategically taking a bathroom break mid class to regain my breath in the bathroom stall in private. I felt tired, out of breath and ashamed. After two weeks I had not built up any exercise tolerance. This made me nervous. I called my rheumatologist and got an appointment for late June, which was about 4 weeks away. I had always been healthy, so I really didn't worry.

Whammo- wrong answer-This would be the first of many hard lessons I learned in this journey. Within a few days it became clear that I needed a doctor and fast. I was in rough shape. I could barely walk around the house without getting completely out of breath, and my abdomen was swollen (and it wasn't from eating!) I called the doctor and asked to see him before the appointment in June. He saw me within a couple of days. My blood pressure was insanely high for someone who had never had an issue with blood pressure at 170/110, and an x-ray showed that my heart was enlarged. My physician immediately ordered me into the hospital. There I received the first of many lessons in what I liked to call "How To Be a Patient."

The lining around my heart had fluid around it (pericarditis), a complication of the scleroderma. They drained it with a big, HUGE needle, and of course I couldn't help but watch. I watched with an odd mixture of fright and detached interest. Apparently, it was interesting to the staff as well; I think there had to be about 11 or 12 people jammed into the room, watching the procedure go down.

I guess this procedure, a pericardiocentesis, is not done that often, especially not to young people, so I was particularly entertaining. I think I felt pretty comfortable saying that I was now a Professional Patient.

There I was, naked, in front of a dozen people, when one of them accidentally touched one of the sterile items from the kit that was to be used during the procedure. As a result, they needed to get all new sterile equipment, which took at least 30 minutes. (I guess they couldn't locate the correct kit either.)

All the while I lay, naked, trying to have some type of absurd conversation with a bunch of strangers.

-- Liz

And so the transformation to Professional Patient began: with me at first being kind, naive, cooperative, and accommodating.

That would change quickly.

If that episode of equipment contamination had occurred a few years, even a few months later, the first thing I would have done would likely be to kick everyone out of there and ask for a robe to cover up. Next, I would have asked how long of a delay we were talking about—I was hungry! Too bad if they had to re-sterilize me and everything else, please get me something to eat (all, still very nicely, of course.) Last, I would have everyone sign papers indicating exactly what he or she would be doing during the procedure and who exactly would be doing it.

I am a slow learner, or quick learner, depending on your perspective.

After that event, I was led to believe by my doctors that the crisis was over. I would heal and go about my life. I was on a leave of absence from work, and really truly believed that I would be returning to it soon.

I would never return to work again.

Slowly, over the next few weeks, I realized I was not really getting better. The first year alone would bring 8 more hospitalizations, each one lasting a week or more.

I was still very out of breath and could not walk very far. I took more tests.

I went to see the cardiologist for the results. I went by myself, not thinking much about it. He told me outright, I am very sorry, Liz, you have Pulmonary Hypertension. He paused and asked, "You do know what that is?" I nodded. I did know. I had read the literature. Often Pulmonary Hypertension happens to people with Scleroderma over the course of their illness. But the process, I thought, could take many years. Generally it follows a progression of mild, moderate and then finally, severe.

I was not prepared for what the Doctor said next, "You have Severe Pulmonary Hypertension. I am sorry. I feel sorry for you." Maybe 2-5 years prognosis, he added. I left stunned and furious. "I am sorry? I am sorry??" That was all he could offer me? I was so angry, that that was all he had to say, I never returned to see him again.

Granted at that time, in the year 2000, Pulmonary Hypertension was a relatively hopeless disease, a disease I would later nickname "Evil Disease Extraordinaire". But to end the conversation with 'I am sorry' was just too much for me to bear. There could have been any number of ways to end a gruesome conversation on life expectancy in a more hopeful manner.

He could have referred me to Pulmonary Hypertension specialists who deal with this illness exclusively and can help you better understand what you are facing. Or perhaps, suggest a particular hospital that is doing extensive research on Pulmonary Hypertension. Or maybe assist in finding an organization, support group or online resource (of which there were many, I would soon learn) to help a person. There were many options that would not cut off hope at the kneecaps.

Science, technology and medicine changes so rapidly that what may be true today may be completely wrong and outdated 5, or even 2 years from now. Research quickly becomes outdated, often before it is published. The changes I have seen in the last 10 years in the treatment of Pulmonary Hypertension alone are astounding.

Hope can never be bad thing…

Monday, December 17, 2001
The power of gratitude is a very intense thing. Gratitude, appreciation, thankfulness, blah blah… those words mean nothing. UNTIL THEY MEAN SOMETHING.

Then watch out.

I have been astonished and amazed at the amount of giving I have seen in the past year and a half. People have given their time, their hearts, their love, their skills, and financial help, all unselfishly.

People have given emotionally by calling, hugging, talking, and crying.

People have given in concrete ways by cleaning, shopping, cooking, and doing laundry. Family and friends have given us so much, and they continue to surprise me.

They give…. they ask, they give more. It warms my soul, and it gives me an understanding of 'giving' that I never knew before.

Being sick has given me the opportunity to really see and understand what unselfish giving truly is.

I learn from it, and hope that sometime I will have the chance to be 'the giver' and not 'the receiver'.

I would be honored to behave the way I have seen others behave. Isn't that a nice thing to think about human nature????

-- Liz

Thursday, December 27, 2001

People say to me often, 'you are so brave'. I always thank them and then remind them that no, I am not so brave. I just see no other alternative at this time in my life. I am a mother of two young girls; I will fight until there is nothing left to fight. I need to be a mother.

That is one of the many reasons there is no doubt in my mind when it comes to the transplant. Of course there is risk involved, but there are many risks in life, every day.

I also see how quickly I have deteriorated; I know how fast this disease can take my life. I won't give it up without a fight. I have been fighting a long time now, but my resolve is still strong with the hope of the transplants.

I have to admit that at times during my illness where my resolve hasn't been so strong. Not that I ever wished death. But when I felt terrible, and very, very sick, I was very close to understanding what it is to surrender and take your last breath. I sometimes wanted to accept it. The pain and sickness were so overwhelming; they left little brain time for anything else. I did believe I was close to the end, even though I never 'wanted' to be.

When I was first diagnosed, and that doctor who diagnosed me as having Pulmonary Hypertension said 'I feel sorry for you'. I never went back to him again. Not because he was wrong or unkind, but because that was not the answer I needed to hear. I didn't need pity, I needed knowledge. That is what has always driven me--Knowledge.

So off I went to NYC to get the help I needed to survive. The first help was Flolan (I'll write more about that later) and the second help was Viagra. Yes, Viagra (and yes, I'll talk more about this, too!). The pain of the decision-making process has always been tortuous for me. But making literal life or death decisions has really taken the fear right out of my life. Add to that all the little life lessons I have learned along the way and in the end, I have basically had 'fear' essentially beaten out of me. Actually that is not entirely true--I could never be so bold as to say I have no fear. But my supply closet has definitely dwindled away.

It's nothing I want to 'stock up on' anytime soon either.

-- Liz

Practical Advice For A Shitty Diagnosis

⤴

1. Make an appointment with someone who specializes in your specific illness! They may have access to more recent information, relevant research, trials, and other patients (who are always a great resource!). Based purely upon the sheer numbers of patients they see who are just like you, gives them an edge on being better able to help you. (Don't get hung up on what you call this appointment, whether you call it a second opinion, or just learning more about your diagnosis.) Certainly don't get hung up believing you'll hurt your current doctor's (the one who made the diagnosis) feelings. Believe me, he would be running to the same specialist if it were him or his family. This brings me to the next point.

2. Ask your doctor whom he would recommend seeing, or what he would he do if his wife, son, daughter etc. had this illness. *"What would you do?"* is an excellent gauge of what should be next on your agenda.

3. Make more than one appointment, don't be shy! I found a specialist in NYC. Call more than one major metropolitan area if you need to. Maybe you will find that one doctor's next opening is weeks before the other one. Maybe after talking to 2 or 3 different offices and their staff, you'll get a better feeling or vibe from one than the other. Maybe you'll go the first appointment and hate it/him/her, in which case you'll still have another opportunity. Or maybe you go to the first appointment and LOVE it/him/her. You can always cancel the other appointment!

4. Send your medical records beforehand AND also bring a copy with you to the appointment. I can't tell you how many times I have walked into a new office only to have a blank-faced receptionist tell me she has never seen any of my records. CARRY THEM IN HAND. And don't let them keep it either. They are likely to lose them. Offer them a copy. Also, another unfortunate firsthand experience. I encourage you to use any hospital provided websites (my hospital uses "My Chart") to keep track of your data, there also plenty of apps that can help you keep track of your data, your EMR (electronic medical record). Then you have it wherever you go.

5. Make the appointment as early in the day as you can, and as early in the week. They are more likely to be running on time, or at least close to your scheduled time. Getting there early also gives them the opportunity to schedule more tests for you that same day, if need be, which is better than waiting until the next day, or the next week, especially if you are feeling badly.

6. If you are feeling badly or fatigued, don't be afraid, ashamed, or scared to ask for a wheelchair! The layout of bigger hospitals and centers can be very difficult to negotiate. If you need to go to the lab for blood work, then to radiology for an x-ray and then to the clinic and then the pharmacy, save your strength, get a wheelchair! Don't fret if you are by yourself, they have people available to push you.

7. Always check for valet parking. Sure it sounds like a luxury, but you don't need to waste energy finding parking and walking from the parking lot to the building. Generally most places will give you a voucher for free or reduced parking if you have an appointment or are there for treatment (but NOT if you are visiting your Aunt Mary!)

8. Have the contact information of every doctor you see on your cell phone. Include addresses, phone numbers and fax numbers (so that, hopefully, they will share and coordinate your care, but that's a whole other chapter). Sign releases allowing them to discuss your

case among one another! Again, all this will help ensure a continuity of your care.

9. Put all expenses on one credit card/ debit card. These include every insurance copay, medicines at the pharmacy (both prescription and over-the-counter), all expenses involving gas, meals, and hotels if you have to stay overnight. Everything! This way you can keep track of it easily for tax season, and even more importantly you rack up miles at the expenses of your illness! And then, when you are better, you can reward yourself with a treat, or go on an awesome trip somewhere (I went to Greece and Istanbul; yup, that's a lot of miles). Remind yourself often as you go into astronomical debt: *"What a great trip it's going to be!"*

10. Be ready for and (graciously) accept changes! Lots of them. You will need to come to terms with a paramount shift in the way you treat your body; with vast shifts in the way to eat, the way you think and, the way you rest. (Much more on this later)

11. Here is the hardest one of all, Accept Help! When people offer to help you, you may not know how to accept the help. Practice saying "Yes" when people want to help you. This one is so hard for people, me included. I am going to go into more detail later. But for now graciously accept and feel blessed that people care enough to offer.

<u>*Monday, December 31, 2001*</u>
Today is 'tapping' day, what does that mean?

That means that every two weeks since April of 2001, I have gone to the doctor for a paracentesis. What is that?

It is a fancy word for getting the fluid out of my belly. When people suffer from heart failure, they can have many symptoms; one is ascites (fluid in the abdominal cavity). Fluid can build up around any of your organs, such as your heart, lungs, liver etc. In my case it was the abdominal cavity.

I take insane amounts of diuretics, eat a no salt diet, but it just doesn't do the trick. Each time I get tapped, I begin to refill, within a few days. I get swollen, uncomfortable, and by the end up my two-week cycle I usually can't walk or eat much. On top of it all, it hurts.

So every 14 days, I go see the gastroenterologist, and he drains my stomach.

This is no high- tech adventure in modern medicine, I don't mind telling you--It is downright prehistoric.

First, my stomach is numbed with a needle (this is the part that hurts like hell). Next, the doctor inserts a bigger needle, with about 8-10 inches of rubber hose (like a big piece of spaghetti). The noodle is then sunk into my abdomen. Then, the hose is connected to a 2-liter bottle that has a vacuum seal, and off we go.

This takes about 3 to 5 liters of fluid out of me each time (which is a huge amount when you consider I only weigh about 100 pounds). Each liter that is taken weighs about 2 pounds.

I lost about 12 pounds in one afternoon. I felt awful afterwards. Nobody is supposed to lose that much weight in one afternoon, ever!

Anyway, as I said, the process isn't very high-tech; the fluid either comes out, or it doesn't. If it doesn't come out on its own I literally have to roll to my side to drain it and have it all to come out. Gross huh?

It looks like amber beer too. Super gross. Sorry.

At any rate, it's a form of torture that I endure in hopes of a mere 5-6 day respite.

-- Liz

Deconstruction of All Things "Important"

The first year of my illness was the most horrendous. It brought hospitalization after hospitalization, where it seemed I was getting worse and worse each time. All I could do was watch as my old life fell away piece by piece.

First, I could no longer work. Soon after that, I could barely walk around my own house. I could not do simple things like pick up toys or clothes off the ground, as it would hurt my heart and leave me nauseous and dizzy to bend over. I would look at my children's untied shoes helplessly--the effort to get 'there' impossible to convey to anyone. I learned really quick to buy slip- on shoes, Velcro strapped shoes, and clogs, for all of us!

Other simple chores like emptying the dishwasher or washing my hair left me so exhausted and out of breath, that they often required naps afterwards.

The 'fatigue' I felt is impossible to describe to anybody who hasn't experienced it. I was sleeping 16-18 hours a day with hardly a speck of energy to show for it. The only way I can explain it is to imagine that a normal person sleeps and then get a full tank of energy to run on for the day, every day. Well for me, every day (or every other day, or once a week) I got an 1/8 of tank of energy to use, and there was no guarantee after using it-- and after sleeping the next night-- I would get more. It was a rotten way to live, and I learned quickly that even this meager existence required *planning*. For instance, if I knew that on Saturday I wanted to take my daughter to a birthday party, I knew I could not do anything the night before, or plan anything for the day of, or after. Even something as benign as going out to dinner after the party was impossible, as I did not have that kind of energy. It forced me to think and rethink what was important, and what was not important quickly: working, cleaning the house, cooking, laundry, errands = Not Important. Going to birthday parties, soccer games, volunteering, talent shows, school parties, events with family and friends= Important.

January, 2002

⟶

Tuesday, January 8, 2002

I know what it's like to be old. I do. I have never really known a single elderly person for most of my life; I had no grandparents, great aunts, or anything like that growing up. But I know what it is to be old. When I got sick, I slowed right down. I walk slow, eat slow, drive slow, and get change out at the cash register slow. I am 35 years old, but I behave in many ways like the elderly.

But now, I am also aware of the toll it takes; what it's like to be unable to keep the pace with the rest of the world and to suffer through the impatient stares of those traveling at a greater speed (and I don't mean just the highway). It is very difficult to keep the pace and not be 'a nuisance'.

So, I find myself making, I am sure, the same choices the elderly make. I go out in the morning during the week. Forget the weekends and late afternoons. Too many people, too fast, all frustrated with me, until of course they see my IV medication pumps; only then I am granted some kind of immunity for not being able to participate up to speed.

On top of it all, my grace, flexibility and strength are all gone as well. I learned this one the hard way. I went to the mall one day and had just parked the car. There was a raised sidewalk to walk up on to. I missed it and tripped. Anyone else would have tripped and looked like a fool. I tripped, had no control, and could barely get my arms out in time to stop the force. I banged my head, face, shoulders, and scraped my knees bloody. Then I realized I could not get up. People did not come to help me up either, not right away anyway. They just looked at me, I guess, thinking I could get up. I think that when I finally started crying and screaming 'I can't get up', some women came over and helped me up off the concrete.

That devastated me, physically and emotionally. (Never mind that I didn't go back to the mall for a long time either). Scott picked me up and took me home; I immediately crawled into bed, humiliated.

I know the meaning now of "I have fallen and I can't get up" and it's not funny.

I understand what it is to be helpless. I struggle with the loss of independence every day, as I am sure the elderly do.

If I ever receive the gift of growing old, at least I will know how to do it.
-- Liz

Tuesday, January 12, 2002
The journey for these transplants started at Mt Sinai hospital in NYC, where I asked my pulmonary hypertension specialist to refer me to their transplant program. Yes, you read that correctly. With all the doctors I was seeing, not one mentioned transplant as a possible option.

My sister-in-law and I went to meet with the transplant surgeon for an initial interview. We came from Queens to Manhattan by train, which turned out to be a mistake. The train stop is about 5 blocks away from the hospital, which I knew would be difficult to manage due to the severity of my illness. I just didn't realize how hard it would be. Two blocks into my walk, I was completely out of breath. And by out of breath I mean Out Of Breath -I just ran a mile uphill, because I was being chased. That kind of chest heaving, pain-in-the-side out of breath.

I begged my sister-in-law not to tell my mother what she was witnessing. I cried, not only from the physical pain and distress, but from the defeat. I could envision her telling my mother "She can't even walk a couple blocks anymore "--and then I thought about how upset my mother would be. I made her promise me she would not tell my mother what she saw that day.

Eventually, I would become a lot more savvy about where I could and could not walk. I learned which blocks were flat and which had an incline. And most importantly: I learned to take a cab. I would take a cab even for distances as short as 4 blocks. And yes, it was embarrassing getting in a cab for that length of time. Cab drivers would give me strange looks. I knew that they couldn't understand what I was doing, some thought I did not know where I was going and politely they would point out, "but Miss, that address is right up on the right".... Generally whomever I was with would be quick to point out that I was sick and could not make such distances. I couldn't care less what people thought, as I didn't have even an extra ounce of anything to explain away my odd behavior.

Finally, we made it to the hospital, and surprise, surprise--the distances in hospitals are also difficult to negotiate. Later, I would learn to ALWAYS take a wheelchair in a hospital, but that day I was not so enlightened. I walked. I was exhausted. The walk from the subway to the hospital and then to the office would take any normal person 12-15 minutes easily, took me 40 painful minutes with stops.

The transplant surgeon listened to my medical history while I coughed and coughed, unable to catch my breath from the walk there. He told me right then and there that I was not a candidate, given my history of scleroderma and my current symptoms. Scleroderma, he explained, could not be cured with a transplant; therefore it could be seen as a possible "wasted resource". As he listed all the reasons why I wasn't a viable candidate, the tears ran down my face. By the time he wished me all the best and I reluctantly shook his hand, I had my next plan formulating.

I went home and spoke with my other sister-in-law; she called for information on other transplant centers.

At that time Pittsburgh, Texas, and California were the only places that would consider me, given my Scleroderma. I set up an evaluation with the transplant team in Pittsburgh.

When I was evaluated in August, the transplant team in Pittsburgh determined that I needed two lungs. At that time, they were concerned about my weight, and wanted to try new medication for my heart failure. When they asked me to come back a month later, my status had changed. Apparently, the damage that occurred to my heart in those few weeks had been severe. They no longer thought that the lung transplant would be sufficient.

Then I received the most bizarre letter EVER from my insurance company-- probably in the history of modern American society for that matter. My insurance company denied the lung transplant, saying that given my test results, I needed a heart along with the lungs.

"Based upon the medical records provided to us… we cannot authorize a double lung transplant…double lung transplants are medically necessary for increased pressure in the lungs with recoverable heart impairment. After reviewing the information received, this member would benefit from a heart lung transplant and not a double lung transplant. Therefore the request for a double lung has been denied."

At least they were both arguing the same point, I thought.

When I returned to the hospital, they set me up with the IV medication, and insisted that I begin stomach tube feedings. I agreed to the IV, but asked to wait on the stomach tube.

I cried. I could not bear the thought of another tube coming out of my body. How could I parent, physically, with tubes and cords all getting tangled up all around me, all the time? I begged the doctor to let me try to gain weight on my own. I was weighing in at 98 pounds with fluid. He shook his head told me not to hold out too much hope--that he had seen many others before me that were unable to keep the weight on, and then became too ill for transplant.

But I couldn't do it, not yet anyway. It was a tortuous decision. The following day, the doctors thought that perhaps I should not go home at all--that perhaps it was in my best interest to stay in the area, where they could monitor me until my transplants came.

That was when I officially lost my mind... How could I possibly stay in Pittsburgh so far from home? Stupid thoughts like "who's going to dress the kids for school?" entered my mind.

I wept and told the doctor that there really was no chance that I could stay; that I needed to go home and be a mother. I basically cried and begged my way out of there. I agreed to come back in another month and then, if I had not gained the adequate weight, I would let them insert the feeding tube. I went home and ate as much as my body would allow. I was able to gain a couple of pounds. That was October. This is January, and I have gained another 5 pounds since then. Can you imagine if I had stayed there?

--Liz

I couldn't even begin to fathom what would have happened to me if I had stayed in Pittsburgh. I know instinctively that I would have never survived. For me, my daily motivation was my children, regardless of how little I could actually do for them. They were truly the reason I bothered to try to get up, move, or even breathe for that matter. And to think that the doctors wanted me to be closer to *them*, rather than my children!

I know I would have never survived the stay there--literally--without my girls. But the doctors did not understand that. As a result, I started to live with the fear that the decision I made would be enough for the doctors to label me "non-compliant"--the worst thing a patient could be labeled, particularly a transplant patient. Only "compliant" patients are considered for transplant.

Somewhere, somehow along the way this term became transformed into "unworthy" by healthcare professionals.

Between not wanting the feeding tube and not wanting to stay in Pittsburgh, I was sure to be labeled "non-compliant", a medical Scarlet Letter, a definite "no-no" for anyone waiting for an organ. But the boundary for me was separation from my children; and, as I said before, they were the reason for me trying to survive--and therefore *any* talk of separation from them was off limits.

Wednesday, January 16, 2002

> *"Dying is easy it's Living that scares me to death"*
> *-ANNIE LENNOX*

Thursday, January 17, 2002

I have a Hickman catheter; it is part of my high maintenance medical routine. I change my medicine daily. But first I have to mix it. The process takes about 45 minutes a day. Depending upon the amount of maintenance, sometimes I just have to change the medicine. Some days, I have to replace the lines and change my dressing.

What's a Hickman? Basically, it's a tube that connects my medicine to my heart. Tubes run up the side of my body and they go in right above my right breast. I have a double Hickman (two tubes). It's connected to 'My Bag' as I affectionately call it, or my medicine. Imagine a small purse with a brick inside, that's what it's like.

I cried terribly the day they put it in. Not because I didn't think I needed it, or because it requires constant daily attention, or EVEN because it tethers me down (literally) but because when they inserted it, I was only on one medicine, Flolan. I couldn't understand why I needed two lines. As a matter of fact, they inserted the darn thing because they could not find the single lumen (one tube) in the operation room at the time. I was already under the knife, so to speak when they said they "couldn't find it".

The surgeon said, "Say ow" I said "ow". She said "No really, say OW like you mean it!" So I screamed "OW", and she stabbed me in the chest with the end of the line. That's how I got stuck with a double. I wept.

That was Sept of 2000, and by September of 2001, they added another IV anyway. Dobutamine was added for my heart failure. Now I have two small purses with two bricks in them. I didn't have to go through any traumatic procedures though. I was very thankful; almost grateful. They just hooked me up and monitored me.

I guess sometimes a moment in our lives that we think is disastrous really is not. Depends on what angle you look at it and when.

-- Liz

<u>*Monday, January 21, 2002*</u>
I love eating, I always have, and I have always been petite. In the past, people have always marveled at my "eating abilities".

Of all the losses I have suffered, I suppose the loss of my appetite and eventually the daily nausea, has been pretty tough on me. I used to wake up motivated well, not to start the day…but to start to eat. Eat.

Wings, Salsa and chips, Wine, My mother's cooking, Scott's cooking, a Very Large bag of salt and vinegar chips, Salami and of course everyone's favorite, chocolate.

All, "Off the menu".

People have always respected my zest for food too. It is how I love to socialize, it is one of the reasons I love my husband (he was a chef you know).

Once, I had to throw my coworkers out of my office to eat a Cream Puff larger than my head. For real. I needed them to get out, give me privacy; the cream puff was that good. They still laugh about that to this day.

I Love food and I take it seriously. There were about five months last year where food did not appeal to me; it made me nauseous to eat. My diet consisted of a glass of milk, noodles and butter. It was a time where I felt truly robbed and angered. What a bitter irony to not be able to eat when you love food so much.

Lately I have been luckier-- my appetite is good, I crave food and enjoy it again wholeheartedly (no pun intended). I just can't eat everything I'd like to eat, but at least I can enjoy it.

Whew!

-- Liz

Wednesday, January 23, 2002

> *"The ultimate measure of a man is not where he stands in moments of comfort and convenience, but where he stands at times of challenge and controversy."*
> -- DR. MARTIN LUTHER KING, JR.

Thursday, January 24, 2002

I am very excited about getting my transplants. I am scared to death about getting my transplants. I am hopeful, fearful, and terrified. Everything, all at the same time.

Really, I can't wait. The prospect of a better life almost makes me giddy at times. Every day I think, today could be the day. Every day I wish that it could truly BE 'the day'. OK, I admit, maybe not every day. Some days when the weather is awful, icy or snowy, I pray that the call does not come. I am scared to death that I'll get The Call, and I won't be able to make it out of the Binghamton airport. I am not sure what I would do if I missed my transplant because of "inclement weather". It makes waiting in January for a transplant pretty difficult.

-- Liz

Tuesday, January 29, 2002

The American Heart Association has heart classifications. This information is used to determine some important things, like functional ability and prognosis. They range from class I- class IV. As you can imagine I am classified a class IV, even though some days though I can feel like a class III.

This classification was used to give me my official title of "disabled. It was a very hard title to receive, certainly not one that people generally strive for, or are envious of.

Anyway, I had to take this official documentation to the town office building, to verify my disability, and receive my disabled parking tag. I had no problem; they filled out the necessary information and gave me my tag. On it, it had an expiration date, which I thought was kind of ironic and funny given my slightly twisted and dark sense of humor. But as soon as they wrote the number March 31, 2004, I started to cry, thinking that the damn tag would be "effective" probably way longer than I would. The poor people at the town office building didn't know what to say. I certainly did not have the words to explain either. So with my eyes full of tears, I grabbed my then 4-year- old's hand, and ran out of the building (or, my rendition of running at least). Tough day.

-- Liz

February, 2002

⟋⟍

Friday, February 1, 2002

I am not sure about what a happy or a fulfilled life is. I don't pretend to know or understand the basis of human fulfillment. I am not a philosopher, nor do I pretend to be. But I do know that it is the search for meaning and joy that makes us human. This is what separates us from other animals. We've known that forever and still can't seem to get it "right".

I struggle with it pretty regularly. Popular psychology tells us to live simply, with acceptance, and to live for each day. As a society, we (or many of us anyway) try to live by this mantra. But it doesn't work, and as humans we're always left searching for more and better, feeling unfulfilled and empty. We are left trying to settle for what we have. Some can graciously accept what has have been given on their plate.

I personally know what it's like to settle for what I have, because I have been in the position of having nothing, or almost nothing left. I have looked at life from the deep dark bottom. I have been physically and emotionally devastated by my illness. I know what it is like to have no energy, no breath, no desire. I have seen this "bottom"; it isn't a very good place.

So not only will I settle for anything I am given, but I will like it. Would I like more? Definitely; I truly believe it is our nature as human beings to want more, but I will take it--you bet I will.

To help me deal with the hand that I have been given, I use a metaphor that involves food (imagine that!). We all eat. Every day. We need to eat. We have to eat. It is how we live. We are served our meals each day. We can choose to be grateful for the meal we receive however grand, mediocre, or poor it is--or not. That is our choice. But that is what will fill us.

Perhaps in life we can't choose all our meals, but at the very least I believe we can choose the ingredients that our meal will be made of. And if we are cooking with rotten ingredients and expect something other than a rotten meal, well then silly us. Too many of us kick, scream and whine when our meal is delivered. We feel cheated.

I have decided that it's not about the meal. It's about the ingredients that make the meal. It makes the meal something we want and savor. Who cares if it's "Spaghetti O's"?--if you love it, then treasure it, and savor it.

I have promised myself that I will do my best to never feel that "the grass is greener". But at the same time, that's not to say I won't have a pity party for myself every now and again. I will never believe that I am "settling" for a lesser life, because I know there is so much more.

I guess what I am saying is that not only will I take whatever life doles out to me, but I am also going to like it, love it, treasure it, be ever grateful, and savor it.

I am choosing the ingredients for my delicious entree.

-- Liz

<u>*Monday, February 4, 2002*</u>

> *"The mind is its own place, and in itself, can make heaven of Hell, and a hell of Heaven."*
> *-- JOHN MILTON*

<u>*Wednesday, February 6, 2002*</u>

Last week I had the opportunity to go to the BBC Concert Orchestra at the Anderson Center. My friends called--they had an extra ticket, and asked me to join them. I hesitated for two reasons; First, I don't usually go out at 8pm, because it is too late for me. The second reason was the music. Sometimes loud music is enough to make my heart hurt--literally. But I decided to go and give it a try.

It was just lovely. The music was as sweet as could be. After the first piece I asked my friends what instrument they would play if they could play anything. One thought she would like to play the cello; she had learned some as a child, and loved the sound of the cello. Another friend and I both decided that we would have to play percussion. You know the guy that smashes the cymbals together? That's me – all the way. It is an instrument that stands alone, and the percussionist gets to play the most intense parts of the piece. We decided it is the exclamation point (!) of the orchestra. We agreed that we would like to be the exclamation points. Furthermore, since I do tend to have ADHD-like qualities, I thought that playing something like the violin would be out of the question. I would have to sit for the entire performance, amongst many other violinists, and make sure I was constantly in tune with the rest of the ensemble, and on the same page. I thought, no way, I couldn't do it. I couldn't sit with the masses. It's (!) for me. We laughed.

Intermission came. We chatted some more, and the theatre was packed with probably about 1500 people; the orchestra itself added another 50. We saw two men in tuxedo tails approach us. We asked if they played in the orchestra, they nodded and then laughed at us. Really who else would be wearing tails to a performance? While we were busy feeling stupid, they introduced themselves to us. They were The Percussionists.

Of Course they were. We laughed so hard.

They didn't understand what was so funny, and we certainly couldn't explain it. The irony of it all was just enough to keep us giggling our whole way home.
-- Liz

<u>*Saturday, February 9, 2002*</u>
There have been times while I have been sick that I have been 'chronically ill', and there have been times when I have been 'terminally ill'. There is a difference, I can tell you that. Both present their own challenges.

Living with a chronic illness means just that: I am living with illness. Been there. This means I make room in my life for all the things that being sick means. If I have to rest or lay down for 16-18 hours of each day...well then that's the way it got to be. Sometimes I can adhere to that. Sometimes I am just downright stubborn. I don't want to give up all the things I had. So I end up doing what I want to anyway.

Then I pay the price. Sometimes I don't do anything and still pay the price. But that is the way it is with Pulmonary Hypertension. It is insidious that way--attacking with no real rhyme or reason. This makes it a terrible disease to accept because it is just beyond the scope of control, and that's frustrating. But I can live with it. It's just not as fun as my old life.

Now, living with a terminal illness means that I am dying from my illness. Been there, too. I have witnessed the process of death within myself; watched as it slowly took more and more away from me. This is tremendously painful for a lot of reasons. The biggest reason: grief--my own, and the grief of others. Watching my family and friends grieve, with me there grieving every bit of the way with them. That is some truly very tough stuff. I live with my reality every day; but for many others, it is a seriously tough place to visit. I know how it can make some squirm, because it makes ME squirm.

Dying slowly is no picnic. As matter of fact, it is a definite form of torture. Watching my mother, as she desperately tries to understand why I was "struck" by this disease is…Hell. No mother should ever have to watch their child wither away.

Everyone—including me-- tries to put their best foot forward during this time in my life. Well, let me tell you what I learned from this experience: I'd rather get hit by the ol' proverbial bus. People can say it has to do with attitude, or being positive or whatever…but the bottom line is, when you can't muster up the breath to speak, or the strength to change your position while lying down, you have bigger problems than your "attitude".

Either way is hard.

-- Liz

<u>*Tuesday, February 12, 2002*</u>

I think that the year 2001 could be officially considered the Worst Year of my Entire Life. Let me rephrase that: I'd like to think that the twelve months of 2001 were the worst of my life. I suppose there could be a worse year coming up around the bend, but I am just going with 2001 was the worst year of my life.

In January 2001, I had just finished 6 months of chemotherapy on the drug Cytoxan, in hopes that it could stop the lung fibrosis that was occurring due to the scleroderma. I had two more pericardiocentesis (taking fluid out from around my heart) done in December and January, and I could still barely breathe or walk. I ended up in the hospital again. The doctors found that the fluid had collected around my heart again, within a matter of days. They decided that a pericardial window--a type of heart surgery-- would be necessary. I was admitted to the Critical Care Unit at my local hospital. The doctors decided that while they were familiar with the surgery here in Binghamton, it should be done in New York City under the supervision of my pulmonary hypertension specialist.

That morning they made their decision: They would have to transport me by ambulance, the trip being over 3 hours long. I am pretty unsure about dates and times, given the huge amount of stress my body was under. No wonder I don't remember much! I think I was in the hospital for about 17 days.

But what I do remember is: I was waiting for the ambulance drivers to pick me up at the hospital; the first crew showed up hours later than anticipated and was not adequately credentialed to take me. I guess someone needed to be a critical care specialist or something to that effect. The next crew showed up hours after that. We finally left.

It was mid-January in upstate NY--dark and raining. Due to regulations, Scott was not allowed to ride in the ambulance; he had to follow right behind us the whole way down. I had to lie down in the stretcher--not the best way to travel for a dizzy and nauseous patient.

We had to pull over on the side of the highway because the ambulance driver's phone had no batteries. We had to sit on the highway waiting for their backup to deliver batteries. Later, they asked me if I was thirsty; I said I could use some water, assuming they had it in the ambulance. They were very kind to me. But we had to get off the highway again to stop for drinks.

I was starting to smile, this was becoming a debacle. But then it got even funnier. They got lost. Somehow we had missed the proper exit in our search for water and the two ambulance guys were arguing in the front over a map. I asked to look at the map, and then because I grew up in NYC, I was able to tell them exactly where we were going. I lay in the back of the ambulance holding up the map, telling them exactly where to exit and what lanes to get in.

The moment was not lost on me, I laughed really hard. I was in ambulance, lost, in New Jersey--this was hilarious. Hilarious. Then, I told them where to get some good pizza before they headed back.

My husband and I still laugh about that day.

-- Liz

<u>*Thursday, February 14, 2002*</u>
For Valentine's Day:

> *"The bottom line is that people are never perfect, but*
> *love can be. We waste time looking for the perfect*
> *lover, instead of creating the perfect love."*
> *-- TOM ROBBINS, STILL LIFE WITH WOODPECKER*

<u>*Tuesday, February 19, 2002*</u>
This weekend I had the dubious honor of being on the front cover of my local newspaper. Oh dear, it wasn't exactly how I had envisioned my fifteen minutes of fame. The headline was "Giving Up Is Not An Option". I suppose that's better than 'Mother Of Two Kills Herself, Her Husband And His Lover In A Jealous Rage.'

They did an excellent job given the given the nature of the material. It was tremendously difficult to see and read.

We were away for the weekend. I had doctor appointments in NYC, and then we went to visit my mother for her birthday, so I got to see many of my friends and family. It's a hard trip; it takes a lot of out me, but well worth it.

Anyway, we were in Great Bend, Pennsylvania when we stopped for gas and saw the newspaper at the gas station. My daughter Emma screamed "Mom! We're famous!"

It was pretty funny and bizarre.

Since then, I have had dozens of phones calls, letters, and emails, from both friends and complete strangers. Once again, I have had the opportunity to be amazed by the benevolent spirit that people have and their willingness to give.

People who didn't know anything about me, but read the article, somehow, on some level, connected with me. Maybe they themselves are ill, or they have a loved one that is or was ill. All kinds of people, from everywhere.

I have always understood that there are no rules when it comes to human tragedy. I learned this lesson over and over when I worked as a social worker in mental health. I know that it doesn't take much to cross the line. You can have any one piece of the puzzle taken away (your health, your family, your mind!) and poof…your privilege is gone.

Many people know this, because they have had a piece of their puzzle taken away. Many more learned this on 9/11, when we collectively as a society saw how little it takes to make our whole existence change.

I learn it over and over, with every phone call, letter, gift, flower, donation, or email.

I see how much there is for all of us to be grateful for. Every act of kindness renews my strength, hope, faith, and love. I thank everyone that has "it" to share.

-- Liz

<u>Saturday, February 23, 2002</u>

> *"You gain strength, courage, and confidence by every experience in which you really stop to look fear in the face. You must do the thing which you think you cannot do."*
> *-- ELEANOR ROOSEVELT*

<u>Tuesday, February 26, 2002</u>

The transplant team had many recommendations. Their goal is to get the transplant candidate in the best health possible before the surgery. This way I have the best chance of getting through the surgery and healing. Besides the stomach tube and various other tests, they wanted me to do exercise.

I laughed.

Me? Exercise?? I reminded them that I couldn't walk from my bedroom to the bathroom without turning blue. They said even if I could only do 2 to 5 minutes of walking on the treadmill it would help strengthen me.

I couldn't imagine how I would do that. The nature of my disease is such that when a normal person's blood vessels dilate, mine constrict. So when a normal person exerts themselves, they turn red and sweat, I on the other hand, turn blue and cold. My hands turn blue, my feet, my lips. It's really very attractive. So it comes as no surprise that I am the warmest (and the pinkest) when I do absolutely nothing.

Lying on the couch or in bed actually keeps me warm. Isn't that strange?

Anyway, their idea of exercising did not sit well with me. I started with some stretches and then some strengthening exercises, to improve my flexibility and balance. Finally, I bit the bullet and started riding an exercise bike. At first I could only pedal for literally a minute or two straight…I would get so out of breath and tired. But little by little, I have been able to increase my tolerance to 20 minutes!

That is pretty exciting stuff. Now granted it is not very fast, and I have to take at least half a dozen stops to rest and I oh, did I mention that I never actually power the bike "on"- but I am doing it!

I also took a walk today with a friend. This is huge. Outrageously huge. I haven't actually taken a walk, on purpose anyway, ANYWHERE, in over a year. So really I believe that it's happening. I am strengthening up.

-- Liz

Wednesday, February 27, 2002

So what does it mean when your 5-year-old can recognize and identify songs from the radio? I mean like from a soundtrack to a movie? Emma was listening to a song on the radio and could tell me that it was from the soundtrack of The Wedding Singer. Alright. It's not like knowing a song from The Lion King, or say even, Shrek. OK. So what does that mean when your child can recognize and identify an Adam Sandler movie? What does it say about my parenting? (Yikes)

She heard "You Spin Me Right Round" on the radio in the car, and told me that fact in under two seconds.

I swear we only watched the movie twice. I swear.

But I guess I should have known it was coming when a few weeks ago I caught her on top the coffee table singing, "Do you really want to hurt me/Do you really want to make me cry?…"-- a Boy George/Culture Club song, that also just happens to be on the movie soundtrack to The Wedding Singer …another stark reminder that I am not on my Parental "A-game". Sigh.

-- Liz :)

Waiting for a transplant is more like gambling than a precise medical procedure. It can be many different experiences for different people depending on what organ you are waiting for, how sick you are, and how long you have been waiting.

My experience waiting for two organs--a heart and lung--is actually one surgery. It is removed and reinserted as one piece or "bloc". It comes from one donor and ends up in one recipient. At any given time in the United States there are about 100-200 people waiting for this type of procedure, making it a very rare type of transplant. Of the 200 or so people waiting, approximately 25% will be transplanted within a year. So what does that mean for the other 75%? Well, it means approximately 25% will die while waiting. Another 25% will either get too sick or become too well for transplant. This sounds ridiculous, but the bottom line is that organs are a scarce commodity, and most transplant centers are not willing to let one go to someone who may not survive the surgery. That's the ugly reality, and like it or not, transplant centers are very concerned with their statistics. It is those numbers (as well as other factors) that dictate not only how consumers/patients decide on their transplant center, but which transplant centers can keep their license and stay open for business. Another 25% will wait longer than a year.

In addition to the wait, there are other factors to consider, like blood type. My blood type is "B", which comprises approximately 11% of the US population and is the second-least popular, only behind "AB" with 4% of the population. ("O" and "A" have 45% and 40% respectively.)

It hardly seems fair. Also contributing to the poor statistics are other important factors, such as a person's size. At the time of my transplant, I was weighing in at a mere 95 pounds, making it impossible for me to have anything but a small donor. Why? Because you can fit small organs into a big body, but you can't squeeze large organs into a small body (like mine!). So just knowing that I was waiting for a smaller donor raised all kinds of guilt issues for me, as I began to realize that my donor would most likely have to be a child. Imagine living with that sense of constant hope/ fear/ dread on a daily basis. The angst takes a toll.

Then there is the geographical distance of the donor and the recipient to take into account. You can't have a donor on one end of the country and a recipient on the other end, simply because (most) organs are not viable for that length of time. Lungs specifically have the shortest "shelf life" of all organs.

Lastly, there are other important issues as well; like tissue and antigen match, both of which have to check out in order for your surgery to be a "go".

So what starts out as a medical procedure, ends up more like a karmic Powerball lottery. Very few ever even get a chance.

Thursday, February 28, 2002
It is a very odd thing to wait for a transplant. It is a huge life event that comes with no planning. If you have any type of surgery, you have a date, if you get married, you have a date, if you are pregnant, you have a date (give or take a few weeks!). With a transplant there is no date, there is no set plan, and no bags packed. I mean, really--what do I need for a transplant? Maybe underwear, that's about it. Both Luci and Emma each have a bag packed, they know where it is, and what it's for. I just walk around with a beeper and a list of pilots to call.

I can't imagine how I will physically dial the numbers when the time comes. In the comedic version of my life, I see myself dialing and redialing the wrong numbers...

I talk with the transplant coordinators from Pittsburgh every week, to keep them and myself updated about any changes. They reassure any doubts I may have. Sometimes I just call them up to confirm that I haven't made this whole thing up. They laugh. This week when I spoke with Pittsburgh, they said they actually had a 'b' (my blood type) donor a few days back. The lungs were viable, but the heart was not.

Just knowing this information makes me really nervous. That I was being considered a few days ago makes my head spin. But it also reassures me that it's coming, sooner or later.

Advice for People Waiting for a Deceased Donor Transplant

⟶

- Waiting for the call is one of the hardest things you will have to do. For some it is *the* hardest thing, even harder than the surgery (of course, not for me). The good thing is that at least they can tell you where you are on the list as you start to climb it.
- Get whatever you need in order so you don't have to worry about it. Then realize that no matter what is left undone, it doesn't matter, it can wait. Nothing is more important that your health, so stop sweating the small stuff.
- Make plans! It's great to have things to look forward to. It's OK to cancel if you don't feel well and even better if you cancel because you got "the call".
- Find ways to keep your mind at peace. Whether you pray, meditate, enjoy movies, walks, whatever. Choose the things that bring you peace. (I know, I know. Easier said than done).
- Get sleep. Staying up worrying about things over which you have no control doesn't help you rest. You need to be as healthy as you can be going in to this transplant. Easier said than done, I know. Do whatever it takes, try natural sleep aides, and if they don't cut it, get yourself some prescription sleep medication. Yes, it can be totally addicting (I was addicted for years, but like my doctor said, "You have bigger problems, and you can worry about kicking the addiction after you're well." And I have!)

- Get exercise! I know that sounds absurd and horrific, especially when you can't breathe, but take time to do something, every day. A few minutes on a recumbent bike can do wonders for you! This is direct advice from my Doctor. Remember, you will be lying in a hospital bed after your surgery. "You are going to need to go in there with as much strength as you can to make it through each day". (As predicted, this came in very handy post-transplant when I was hospitalized for over four months.)
- Some days it's good to talk with other people going through the same stuff. They help give perspective and help on the everyday decisions you will have to make. Some days, it's not good to talk to people going thru the same stuff. You will have to decide for yourself, what's good for you on a daily basis.
- Go to the Unos.org website and look at their statistics. They have awesome statistics. Take the time to look at them. This can help guide you to the right hospital for your particular illness and organ! It can help you with waiting times and survival rates, too.
- Make yourself a photo album or collage of the people you love, so that when you are in the hospital you can look at it and smile! It's also nice to share with the medical staff that visits you every day in the hospital. Not only does it give them something to talk about with you, but it helps them see you as a person, a whole person and not just as a patient.
- If you are turned down at one center, find another center that will accept you! Different centers have different protocols. Just because they count you out doesn't mean that you should! What one center may rule out as contraindication, another center may not, and will work with you. They don't all follow the same rulebook. Keep looking. Even if they all say the same thing, you may find that the contraindication that keeps you from having a transplant this year is no longer one the next year because they have found a way to work with it. So if some time has passed since they said "No", try

again. Remember, changes in protocol happen at such a rapid pace, not even the doctors and nurses can keep up with them!

- Which brings me to my last very important point: Do not ever let anyone other than a transplant surgeon tell you that you cannot have a transplant. Regular doctors like your primary doctor, your nephrologist, or pulmonologist, are not as up to date on the latest in the transplant science arena, and are not really equipped to tell people who can and who cannot have a transplant. There, I said it, and I say it again later in the section of advice for health care professionals.

March, 2002

⤴

Sunday, March 3, 2002

I love candy. I eat it every day. One of the side effects of all my medicines is a very dry mouth. Candy helps me make some spit. No chocolate mind you, which I know is bizarre (must be my medication). Just candy, good sugary candy. Give me a gummy worm, I am happy woman.

Ah yes, but Jolly Ranchers are the tour de force in the candy world for me, the piece de resistance. Cherry or watermelon please. Those are my favorite flavors. I buy the variety pack every week at Target. I know, I know, I can buy packets of just cherry or just watermelon, but I don't. (A psychoanalyst could have a field day here.) I buy the variety pack.

I eat the grape and lemon flavors, too. Anyone who knows anything about eating Jolly Ranchers knows that those two flavors are just thrown in there, because really it's all about the apple, watermelon and cherry.

Anyway, I eat the grape and lemon flavors. I don't save them for last, I don't pick through the bag. I eat them right along with yummy flavors. (This is where the therapist could have a field day). Maybe it's because I feel bad for them, or because I don't want to leave them out. Maybe I don't want to discard them- just because they're mediocre or less-than. (Remember charades? Finger on the nose, finger on the nose.)

Or maybe it's just because I want to eat as much candy as humanly possible, all the time.

-- Liz :)

<u>Tuesday, March 5, 2002</u>

Trying to deal with all the emotional complexities of my illness landed me in therapy. I went to a therapist whose focus was chronic illness. One of the things I was challenged to make by the therapist was a "symbol" of my disease.

She suggested I draw, paint, sculpt or create something that would embody my illness. I made my "flip off" ball. What's my "flip off" ball?

I found the "flip off" ball today in my closet. I had forgotten all about it.

You know those tennis like balls that you can throw, but are connected to a string that you Velcro to your wrist? You know, you have seen them demonstrated at the mall or somewhere, I am sure.

Anyway, on the tops of my medicine bottles that I mix each day are little plastic tops that say "FLIP OFF". I glued many of these tops all over the tennis ball. Covered it completely. Of course you have to understand that what I really wanted it to say was something else a little more profane than flip off, but that also starts with the letter 'F'...

The point of it is, that of course when you throw it, it comes right back at you.

More to the point, it comes back harder and faster, the harder you throw it. That is the essence of Pulmonary Hypertension. I can try to throw it away, I can tell it to "fuck off" but the bottom line is that sucker is tied to my wrist; and not ironically, will always come back to hit me with as much force as I throw it.

-- Liz

This brings me back to one of the points I made earlier about changing the way you treat your body. Regardless of what diagnosis you have or have not been given (as is the case with many auto immune diseases), please treat the symptoms that your body is showing you. Do not do "battle" with your illness--that term is misleading, because it implies that you are trying to fight against yourself. You are actually trying to *heal* yourself.

Treat yourself as you would treat a small ill child; with love and compassion, with tenderness. You wouldn't be angry, mad, or tell a small child to buck up and get ready to battle their illness would you? Give yourself the same love you would a child--change your eating habits, say goodbye to your bad habits (you know what they are), and say hello to nutritious and whole foods. Fruits, vegetables, whole grains, beans, nuts, you know the drill. Get rid of all canned and boxed items…nothing "good" comes from them…Make a commitment to treating your body well with love, good food, good rest, exercise-- doing things that make you happy and at peace. Don't think for a minute this is all about what the doctors can or can't do for you. It's very much about what you are willing to do for yourself. So say goodbye to whatever bad habit pains you, for your health's sake. Step up and participate, become a partner in your health. Your doctor can't magically make you better (no matter what any patient or doctor thinks). Take responsibility for your health.

<u>Thursday, March 7, 2002</u>

> *"What lies behind us and what lies before us are small matters compared to what lies within us."*
> *-- OLIVER WENDELL HOLMES*

<u>Friday, March 8, 2002</u>

I ended up in the emergency room today. You know how some people collect frequent flier miles? Well I wish there was some type of "rewards program" for visits to the ER and the hospital. I would be racking it up big time.

Really, I can't complain though, I haven't been there since November, which is a record for me.

I take blood thinners. Lately I have had some problems with bleeding. Often my nose bleeds for hours at time. Today it wouldn't quit. The day was just gorgeous; I wanted nothing more than to breathe some of the fresh warm air. Instead, my daughter was up most of the night and morning vomiting and was home from school. My nose was gushing blood. I waited until my Scott came home from work, and then took myself to the hospital after a couple hours of the bleeding.

I was in the hospital bed, happily eating my box of Runts, when the doctor came in to see me.

He then packed my nose, which is essentially sticking a tampon up your nose-- way up it. It hurt. And then my ear started bleeding. I had to laugh; it was like sticking your finger in the dike.

He asked me all about my medical history, and then informed me that he is a pilot.

He offered to fly me to Pittsburgh when the time comes, if the conditions permit. He gave me his name and number so that I could contact him when the beeper goes off.

So, as usual, something was taken away (the chance to enjoy the beautiful afternoon), but something more important was given.

-- Liz :)

Gradually I would learn to accept things as they are (most of the time anyway!). And to trust that while it may not be my agenda, not in that order or not in that time frame, or not at all, perhaps it was still in my best interest. This was a very hard lesson for me to come to terms with. I needed to trust in the path set forth by the universe (God). That just maybe something good would come from all that I was experiencing. And it did. More importantly, the more I took notice, the more blessings took place in my best interest. The key is to trust and accept that I was right where I needed to be, even if I didn't want to be there.

Wednesday, March 13, 2002
I have suffered many losses at the mercy of my illness. I have grieved over many-- some small (my ability to dance), some medium (my ability to walk), some large (my ability to breathe) and Extra Large (the thought of dying and leaving my family to fend on their own). I still grieve; I imagine I always will. I understand that now. Grief does not go away, it just changes it shape, form, its presentation and its intensity.

The ability to dance is just one of those things I grieve. I love to dance, I always have. Any type of dance. When I was three, I began dance lessons--you know, the standard ballet and jazz type of lessons. Then add the fact that I am Colombian, which in and of itself meant a lot of dancing, all the time growing up. From my family, I learned to cumbia, salsa and merengue. Factor into that the fact that I grew up in Woodside, Queens (which had and still has a large Irish population), I learned to Irish jig with my neighborhood friends. Dance was one of the many life lessons that brought me a very varied and multicultural upbringing.

By the time I was about 11, I was at the School of American Ballet at Juilliard. At that point my classical ballet training was very intense as you might imagine, and I learned that ballet 'all the time' wasn't exactly my cup of tea.

I moved on to other endeavors with a children's repertory theatre, The First All Children's Theatre. There I learned more about musicals, tap and modern dance. My experience with the children's theatre opened many wonderful doors for me. I performed on Broadway and off-Broadway. I had the opportunity to travel with the company and dance in wonderful places like Alaska and China. Later in college, I was able to study and perform in Spain. I was also able to learn flamenco while I was in Spain. Back at school, I continued my education of dance and learned African and even Baroque dance before finishing college.

Later as a mother of small children, I became interested in and taught skills like creative movement to toddlers and preschoolers. I even learned to belly dance. As I continued my work in human services and the helping profession, I decided that the arts were an integral part of healing. I wanted to incorporate the two. My thesis in graduate school was entitled "The Use of Creativity to Foster Resiliency in Elementary School Age Children." One of my last learning endeavors in dance was at the Laban/Bartenieff Institute of Movement Studies in NYC.

When I lost my breath, I lost my ability to dance. It was sad, but not so, so, sad. Because you see, I could watch others dance, and I could enjoy music, and I could always dance inside my head; for that I am very glad. I realized I didn't need a body to dance. Now, I have the gift watching my daughters dance. I cry through each and every one of their performances.

One day not too long ago, my girlfriends and I went out for a girls' night out. In the past this usually meant music and dancing, but since my illness it has meant more passive things like dinner at a friend's house or a restaurant. But I felt up to it. I joined them. They danced and danced. I watched, and smiled, and laughed, until my cheeks hurt. Make no mistake, I was also very sad. It was the first time that I was truly sorry that I could not partake in the festivities. I couldn't join them on the dance floor, but I pulled up a chair and was happy; truly happy.

That night I promised myself--and I made them promise me-- that we would ALL do it again sometime –soon.
-- Liz

<u>*Thursday, March 14, 2002*</u>

> *"The best way out is always through."*
> *-- ROBERT FROST*

<u>*Friday, March 15, 2002*</u>
This week I had some frustrating news dealing with my medical insurance and disability.

Let's see… how do I explain this crazy maze without getting too lost? I will try. The transplant evaluation team evaluates every aspect of you, your physical well-being, your emotional well-being, and your financial well-being.

They tell you how much the transplants will cost, what will or won't be covered, and where you can get any additional assistance if you qualify. It turns out we don't qualify. We don't make enough money to cover the extra costs, yet we are not considered poor enough either. Oh, the irony of it all.

Currently, I am covered by insurance. The transplant is completely covered, but not the immunosuppressants (the medicines I have to take for the rest of my life). They are only covered for about 50%, which translates into roughly $800 to $1200 a month. However, since I am disabled, I do qualify for Medicare, but there is a waiting period. Medicare would cover the transplant, and up to 80% of the cost of immunosuppressants, leaving me responsible for approximately $500 to $800 a month. I don't qualify for Medicare until 2 years have passed from the date of disability (which is obviously ridiculous because if you become disabled- duh you're sick and need medical care).

I become "disabled" in May 2000. Up until now I had thought that my Medicare coverage would kick in this May 2002. Then I found out that eligibility begins 2 years after your first date of payment for your disability. They have a 6-month waiting period before you can start receiving payment. So while I got sick in May, I didn't start to receive benefits until November. November is the date they use to measure my two years.

Ready for the clincher? If I have the transplant before I am eligible for Medicare it will not cover the cost of immunosuppressants-- EVER.

I knew this before. It is the reason the transplant team's evaluation suggested that we begin fundraising. But I thought all I had to do was get to May. Now it is November. To say that I am disappointed is an understatement.

I have contacted the proper elected officials regarding this matter. They say there can be no waiver unless I am in chronic renal failure, that's the rule. My kidneys, thankfully, have always hung in there.

It will not stop me from doing what is best for me either. See, I have this amazingly stubborn will to survive. See my agenda.

Liz's agenda:
1. Get Better.
2. Figure out how to pay for it.
-- Liz :)

Tuesday, March 19, 2002

> "Never seen you looking so bad my funky one
> You tell me that your superfine mind has come undone
> Any major dude with half a heart surely will tell you my friend
> Any minor world that breaks apart falls together again
> When the demon is at your door
> In the morning it won't be there no more
> Any major dude will tell you"
> -- Steely Dan

Wednesday March 20, 2002

There are many emotions that are not accurately or sufficiently described by the words that represent them… **anxiety** is one of those words, I realized the other day--when I realized how much it nag, nag, nags, it tap, tap, taps-- and how it sometimes consumes me. So I looked it up in the thesaurus, to see if there was perhaps another word that could do a more accurate job of describing this general state of being: Nervousness, anxiousness, fear, apprehension, worry, concern, fretfulness, anxiety, fright, panic, alarm, trepidation, dread, terror, uneasy, disquiet. Just a few that I came up with.

But they just don't cut it. Not because they don't properly describe the feeling in a negative way--because the words do that-- they just don't describe how insidious anxiety can really be…

    -- Liz

Thursday, March 21, 2002

Time to talk about Flolan. The drug I love to hate. It is the drug that saved my life. Flolan is what is in "Bag 1". I mix it and change it on a daily basis. It is a powerful vasodilator(widens blood vessels). It is delivered through a pump, and an IV, directly to my heart and lungs. It is powerful; but not potent for very long. So it is delivered continuously, 24 hours, 7 days a week.

What does this mean? The pump is never supposed to stop. I have a backup pump. I have to keep it cold, so I also have to carry around ice packs with it, too.

I once asked the Dr. what exactly would happen if the medicine stopped for any reason, he said, "You know how you blow up a balloon Liz? Then, what happens if you let go, and let the air out? Think of the drug as constantly blowing up your balloon." I got the picture.

The medicine then gets "turned up" so to speak, depending upon my shortness of breath and other symptoms. As I become tolerant of the drug its effectiveness wears out, but the side effects lessen. When I "turn it up", my shortness of breath lessens, but I get kicked in the ass by the side effects. Currently, the pump delivers 37 nanograms of medicine per minute. I started at 4 nanograms. With time I grow tolerant of the dose, and then they turn it up again.

I have to be very careful about infections, I take great care both mixing and changing my medicine. As you might imagine this is no small task in a house with small children. I can only get the site wet when I change my dressing. I change the site dressing 3 times a week, so other than showers, there is no swimming, no baths, no nice hot Jacuzzis (darn!)

So on those three designated days, I shower. The other days of the week, I take a shower with one of those hand-held shower gigs, and I keep it away from my head and chest area. It's a bummer, but as I said, it's all relative in the end really.

When I was hooked up to it, I started with a tiny dose; the side effects are evil, and overdosing on the stuff can literally kill me.

Some of the side effects that I have had, or have, range from mildly annoying to horrendous. They include flushing, or a "Flolan tan" as it called, because it dilates my blood vessels ("Hey Liz you look tan!"), muscle cramps (sometimes so intense and painful I am unable to walk), diarrhea, constipation, nausea, low blood pressure, foot swelling and pain, excessive bleeding (like my nose, and the one time the blood vessels literally exploded in my eye and sent me to the emergency room. We're not talking any small broken blood vessel here), an insane constant rash, and itching all over my body so outrageous that it has literally left me bleeding at times. Then there's facial numbing and jaw pain, too. Jaw pain sounds pretty innocent enough, but it isn't. You know that pain or cramp you get in your jaw when you eat something cold like ice cream? Well, I get that pain in my face whenever I start to chew or eat. And it is not limited to my jaw. More accurately, it should be called face pain, because it hurts whenever I salivate, sneeze, cough, or cry. Whenever I do anything that has to do with my face- it hurts. This of course has a positive spin to it, since it serves as a deterrent from crying. It's no fun to weep if you scream "Ow!" first. Kinda makes you forget what you're crying about in the first place.

It sounds horrific doesn't it? But the tradeoff is breathing and the ability to walk. And that is a pretty serious tradeoff. Ask anyone who has spent any length of time in a wheel chair (and I have had my fair share of being pushed around). It is all about perspective in the end. Really, there is so much I can do with, or without, in exchange for breath.

-- Liz

<u>*Wednesday, March 27, 2002*</u>
Last fall I watched the TV with my eyes wide open and unbelieving. It was the second time in a few months that I watched a tragedy on the news, first was World trade Center and then the American Airlines plane that crashed in Queens killing all the passengers on board. I watched and began to cry. I guess it was more than a cry; it would definitely qualify as sobbing, maybe even crossing over into wailing. At any rate, I could not stop myself. The pain, the victims, their families, I thought.

I couldn't even stop myself for the sake of my children, who had then entered the room.

As I continued to cry, my 5-year old approached me and asked "Mama, why are you crying?" I looked at her and thought of several hundred replies before saying, "Because I am sad. Sad that all those people died". She looked at me with her extraordinary wisdom and said, "But that's OK mom, people die". I looked at her and nodded, "Yes people die- but I guess this was so…unexpected". She consoled me and said, "It's OK Mom; really it's OK…I mean like…sometimes cats die--and it's not even a dog."

I looked at her, smiled, and understood clearly. Sometimes you have to expect the unexpected, which can also be a positive thing.

-- Liz

Sunday, March 31, 2002

This week we are going to Pittsburgh. I have a couple of days' worth of appointments and tests. The girls have never been there. I thought that it was definitely time for them to go, so that they could know where we were going when the time comes, where the hospital is, what it looks like, who the doctors are, etc… just to take some of the mystery out of it and answer some questions. I was relatively certain that it was the right decision when I heard some of the girls' questions:

- How many planes do you take to Pittsburgh? (One sweetie, but we are driving).
- Is it a long trip or short trip? (Long trip baby, about 7 hours).
- Is it hot or cold there? (Whatever it is like here, it is there, maybe a little warmer, but they have 4 seasons just like we do).
- What language do they speak there? (English sweet pea, it is part of the United States).
- Will they give you a new heart when we are there? (No. Not this trip, it is just a checkup).
  And then there is my all-time most un-favorite question of all…
- Doctors don't know everything do they Mom???

As I said, I am relatively certain after making the decision, that it is the right one.

-- Liz

April, 2002

⎯⎯⎯⎯⎯⎯○⎯⎯⎯⎯⎯⎯

<u>Tuesday, April 2, 2002</u>

> *"You don't get to choose how you're going to die,*
> *only how you're going to live. Now."*
> *-- JOAN BAEZ*

<u>Monday, April 8, 2002</u>

I don't deny my illness; I just can't deny my chance for wellness.
We are back from seeing Mr. Heart and Mr. Lung, as my girls refer to my Heart Failure Specialist and Lung Transplant Surgeon.

Sometimes I wish that the doctors could just wave their magic wands, tell me I am cured, and to go home. Then, as I am heading out the door smiling and waving, they could shout, "Hey, don't forget to take out your catheters, before you go to the Bahamas."

I can dream can't I???

The last 5 months have been relatively stable for me. I have gained weight; my ascites and many of the other symptoms that plagued me for such a long time have subsided. My fantasy of course is that perhaps there is a chance that maybe things are changing…

The doctors are happy to see all these improvements and can't explain some of these changes, but their message is clear: This period of wellness is my window of opportunity; they don't want to do anything or change anything that could rock my boat of stability. A line infection or pneumonia could easily take that stability away. They add that my chances of survival now vs. six months ago are much higher (the exact word he used is astronomically).

Recently, I received a scholarship to attend the Pulmonary Hypertension Conference this year in California, but they think I better not go. Too far to travel, they say, at this point in time. So that was disappointing, but not the end of the world.

They believe that my well-being is definitely a product of the intense medication regiment I am on, and that it shouldn't be messed with.

I got their message loud and clear.

So for whatever reason, by miracle or medicine, I am doing well. And this is the time for transplant.

We drove home, relieved that the trip was uncomplicated, and also a little more fearful of what the immediate future holds for us.

-- Liz

Monday, April 8, 2002

> "I'm so tired but I can't sleep
> Standin' on the edge of something much too deep
> It's funny how we feel so much but we cannot say a word
> We are screaming inside, but we can't be heard."
> -- SARAH MCLACHLAN

Wednesday, April 10, 2002 (or, "What I Wrote in Public")

"Liz's Top Ten Fears":

I fear having my cords ripped out of my chest by accident ("Oops! Sorry, Miss I seem to have stepped on your cord!") Alrighty, time to get serious - after all these are fears.

I fear dying before my transplants become available.

I fear dying from a small complication or big mistake made during my transplants or my many hospitalizations.

I fear the trauma of my illness on my children.

I fear getting ill enough to not be able to take care of my children.

I fear getting ill enough to not be able to take care of myself.

I fear leaving my children without a mother.

I fear leaving my husband without a wife.

I fear that my husband will fall in love with someone else while I am still living, (someone healthy and not bedridden).

I fear dying alone, but worse, living lonely.

And the number 1, all time worse fear is that my children will someday have a new mother, and Scott someday will have a new wife, and that all my roles--as mother, friend, love, and spouse will be replaced by a person that I may not like, respect, admire, care for, or approve of.

Ok, ok, it's not so much that I can't count to 10, as much as I have never been really good at following the rules.

Wednesday, April 10, 2002 (What I wrote in private).
My heart is broken, in every way. The story is one of lies, friendship, deceit, betrayal and love, with the existence of some of the things and the lack of others. It involves my husband and my best friend/caretaker, who took care of me in so many ways, and also of my husband, in more ways than one.

Ultimately it is a story of sadness, where I am left knowing some ugly truths about the people closest to me and wondering about the things I don't know.... Scott was home from work, doing chores around the house; he was doing stuff on the computer and baking cookies, when the girls came home from school. I was laying down napping. He got up from the computer to attend to the girls. I got up, sat down at the computer screen and found a note from my girlfriend to my husband. At first, I thought nothing of it-until I read it in its entirety. It didn't say much. It didn't have to. It said just enough for me to understand that everything I thought to be true about my life –wasn't. MY heart sunk to the pit of my stomach and I was utterly and completely devastated, as I reread the simple note in disbelief.

From her:
"The snow is so beautiful, it just makes me even bluer. I want you and need you so much. I want to play in the snow with you. It hurts so bad sometimes, I really feel like I am dying inside. I love you with all my heart, and I want you by my side and in my arms and on my lips....Promise you will love me."

His reply:
"The promise has been made before and will last forever....I love you soooo much."

He says he wants to be here with me, but his heart and eyes tell a different story. I see no love for me and worse, I see his love for her.

I am not sure why he is staying--maybe it is his sense of duty, his loyalty and love for his children. Perhaps the shame of leaving a terminally ill wife.

My soul is damaged.

How do I forgive and have peace of mind?

Can I forgive? What's the point of forgiving Scott if he is going to exist in that faraway place that does not allow us to connect again? Do I have the power and resources to leave a 15-year-old relationship while waiting for the most important event of my life?

Do I torture my children with the pain of separation and divorce on top of having a "sick mom"?

Do I live constantly thinking that my husband is just waiting for me to die so that he can live with his true love happily ever after?

Can I live that way?

How much more can I compromise myself?

Is it selfish to leave? Or do I stay in a mediocre marriage knowing that my Scott has nothing to give me and is in love with someone else?

They both say that it is "love", but I don't think that love is possible when it is created in such a damaging and untrue way. I believe that there were strong and intense emotions, but filling each other's emotional holes and voids does not love make.

Love does not come from lies, pain and hurt....

My suffering seems to have no end. How could two of the most important people in my life, lie to me, manipulate me and play me like they did?

My brother and sister both tell me that perhaps with my new heart will come the ability to love. It sounds corny but it isn't, and I hope with some desperation that it's true, because the old one is damaged beyond repair.

Sadly, I had to revise and rewrite my goodbye letter to Scott:

Scott,

So much has changed since the last time I wrote.

I wish I could say "Well, our love was strong", but I can't.

I wish I could say "We cherished whatever time we had left", but we didn't.

I wish I could say "at least I felt loved and treasured", but I don't.

That's a sorry ass way to have my life end. I sincerely hope it's not the case, but it seems that from our perspective as a couple there will be no "cherishing the moments that we have left together".

In the two years of my illness there has only been sadness, frustration, pity, anger and ultimately a betrayal that broke my heart and damaged my soul.

I doubt very much the chances of a "they lived happily ever after" I am not sure it's possible to recoup the losses at this point in time.

I am sorry you ever fell in love with someone else while I was sick and still living. It was so much easier to say goodbye and wish you the best, including the chance to love and re-marry. It's harder now that I know exactly who it is that you love and wish you could be with.

There is nothing I can do about your love for her, but I will say this. I don't want her in my house or home, near my children EVER, for ANY reason. She is not "allowed" to be with my children as far as I am concerned. She does not have the 'right' to replace me. She (and you) treated me like insignificant dirt by choosing (yes, it was a choice) to love each other.

You couldn't wait for me to die. Rather, you should have waited for me to die. Now I have to live with these feeling and even worse, I have to die with these feelings.

It's not what I want, nor do I know how to resolve it. I know it won't magically go away.

Honestly, I can say that our relationship and the way you have treated me over these past few years was more painful than ALL MY ILLNESSES COMBINED. That is a very harsh but true reality,

Liz

During that horrible time, I acknowledged to myself that there was a part of me that was "trapped" by circumstances--the fact that I was sick, needed health insurance, did not work or have money of my own. I was not independently wealthy. Furthermore, I was not going to intentionally see my children less, by having them split their time between parents, and I was not going to induce more pain upon my children by separating from my husband. My reality, or so I thought at the time, was that I had little time left on this earth. I could not "leave" even if I wanted to. I made the tremendously difficult decision to forgive Scott, for the sake of myself, my health, my children, our friends and my family. I learned a ton about forgiveness (I could write a book). Most importantly, I learned that forgiveness is an ongoing process, a choice that requires frequent (sometimes daily) attention. It took many years of "active forgiving" to move on and forward.

I eventually forgave my girlfriend as well, although that took much longer; and she is no longer part of my life.

At any rate, the person I am now would never list her top ten fears, only her top ten dreams.

For the record, my top 10 dreams:

I will be able to walk (and breathe) someday and it will be effortless.

I will be able to take my children to the park and play with them, even run after them.

I will see my children graduate from high school.

I will be able to care for my family, cook, clean and make their daily life easier.

I will be able to travel with my family to places faraway.

I will take my girls to Colombia South America to meet their cousins and visit with my Dad.

I will go out dancing.

I will take dance lessons and perform again.

I will have a dog, because I can walk him!

I will live a peaceful, joy filled and happy life.

Thursday, April 11, 2002

> *"Sometimes our light goes out but is blown into flame*
> *by another human being. Each of us owes deepest*
> *thanks to those who have rekindled this light."*
> *-- ALBERT SCHWEITZER*

On to much lighter subject matter...many people have been asking about the next fundraiser.

Creative Dance Elements, where my daughters Luci and Emma take dance class, will be holding a fundraiser for my family and me.

"Good Things", a multimedia performance will be on May 18th, 4:00 & 7:00, at the Forum Recital Hall. This is a family event. Featuring original dance choreography of "Turning Lemons into Lemonade"...Dance, music, cinematography, prose...silent auction, raffles and refreshments.

I will be there of course, unless I have better things to do (like fly to Pittsburgh!)
-- Liz :)

<u>*Tuesday, April 16, 2002*</u>
I think I will shave my arms before my transplants.

Shaving my arms will give me something to do while I am in the hospital. That is, watching the hair grow back in.

I guess I'll shave my legs then to, really as a courtesy to all the people who will be taking care of me. The truth is, having had lots of hospital experience (and a very hairy body); I know that it is in my best interests to shave. All that hospital tape can be very, very painful.

So I went out and bought razors. Lots of them.

Maybe, somehow I can shave off the disease? Guess Not.

But God only knows, I wouldn't want any unsightly hair during my surgery.
-- Liz

<u>*Thursday, April 18, 2002*</u>
This week a "dinner crusade" was started in my daughters' school for us. We have been the extremely fortunate recipients in this "culinary adventure", and once again, I am touched by the generosity of strangers.
-- Liz

By the way, this dinner crusade did not last weeks or months, it continued for **years** with our friends and neighbors taking superb care of us. We were so grateful and our fridge always full. Funny enough though, even till this day my kids won't touch lasagna. Apparently they had enough to last a lifetime.

<u>*Friday, April 19, 2002*</u>
This week waiting for my transplants has been more difficult. There are so many emotions that come with waiting, that sometimes it just becomes too intense. This week has been one of those weeks for me.

Waiting for a transplant often means hoping for a donor and well, hoping for a donor means ~ hoping for a donor. Hoping for the right person to die. And no one likes to think about that. It leaves me feeling really guilty.

I know in my heart and soul that becoming a donor is not about dying. It is about giving. It is the ability to share life. That is a huge and wonderful gift.

But the guilt is always there, tapping at the back door...guilt for the donor, guilt for the donor's family who has to cope with their loss and guilt for the other patients who are also waiting.

So I try to remember that it is a gift. And I know that it's a gift that wouldn't be wasted on me. I know that I would put it to good use. That gives me some consolation.

-- Liz

<u>*Tuesday, April 30, 2002*</u>
Strangely enough, being less sick (or more well!) does have some troubling aspects— like, the luxury of thought.

When I am sick, I can only focus on the here and now--the present, what I am doing at this moment, and how I am going to get to the next moment. Pain offers that consolation; there is no time, nor brain space, for objective thought about the past or the future. It gives only one tense: the present.

With wellness comes the ability to judge, ponder, and in general freely think about all that has happened. And guess what? It's painful-- surprise, surprise!

Often, in retrospect I remember certain pieces of space and time that pain and illness did not allow me to earlier...

It can be very distressing; I think more distressful sometimes than the actual moment in time. Because then, I was busy being too sick to care.

I remember one morning feeling really sick. It was a school day and Scott was at work. I woke up feeling really, REALLY sick. So sick, that it is impossible to translate the feeling of "sickness" into words.

For instance the sentence "I woke up coughing and throwing up" does nothing to really describe the actual experience: At that point in time it was not uncommon for me to cough, choke to the point of gagging, and then finally throw up.

We are all familiar with the experiences of "coughing" and "throwing up". This is not like those experiences.

Throwing up is generally thought of as an expulsion from your body, right? Something is poisoning your body and your body is ridding itself of it, right?

Well this is different. This is not your body rejecting anything but itself. There is no food or alcohol poisoning, no virus, no chemo, no bug--just your body shutting down. Saying I quit.

I knew that, on that day. The vomit was shooting out of my mouth. I couldn't get to the bathroom. I couldn't even get something to vomit in. The best I could manage was to sit up, and even then I just threw up all over my bed, the bedroom curtains and myself. (Sorry about the graphic detail.)

I called my husband and told him what was going on; he told me to hang up and call 911.

I did.

I then woke the girls up, told them to get their clothes on for school. Then while conducting the infamous sock search for the day, I returned to my bedroom and threw up some more. I returned and informed the girls that within a few minutes they would be hearing an ambulance and that it was coming to our house, to get me, and that it would be loud. I wasn't feeling so good, is how I explained it to them. I reassured them that I would be going to the hospital, and that the doctors would take care of me there. I cheerily added that they would be having breakfast at my neighbor's house that morning, as if it were some kind of extra bonus treat for them. (But alas they are just young, not stupid; they knew exactly what was going down.)

My neighbor helped me finish dressing the kids; I packed my medicine as the ambulance and the EMTs arrived.

I remember the fear in all us at that moment, and how those kids looked at me before heading to the neighbor's house for "breakfast". And for me, that moment feels more tragic now than it was then.

-- Liz

May, 2002

✎

*B*elieve it or not, many positive things have happened as a result of my illness. I try to always remember that. One of those things is the amount of people~ family, friends and total strangers that have become donors. As a result of my illness and my website, they now see and understand the importance of becoming a donor. People tell me of their conversations with their loved ones. They tell me they have signed their donor card. It is one of the (many) gifts that has come from my illness.

I read somewhere once, that one donor can save up to 8 lives. That's pretty amazing when you really consider it.

In New York, they have made it a very simple task. You can register at the DMV when applying for your driver's license.

Very simple. Very amazing.

I also read somewhere that eyes and heart are the least-donated organs because people feel that they are the windows to the soul, and that that's were a person's soul, or "essence" is.

I also know that 63 people receive transplants each day. 18 people die each day waiting...

-- Liz

Tuesday, May 7, 2002

> "Healing is embracing what is most feared; healing is
> opening what has been closed, softening what was hardened
> into obstruction, healing is learning to trust life."
> -- JEANNE ACHTERBERG

<u>*Thursday, May 9, 2002*</u>

I think that if I were to take a poll of nurses who work in a hospital, they would all agree that how a patient wears their hospital gown is a definite indicator of how sick or well the patient is. Let me explain here—

In my experience as a "professional patient" (to be read with all kinds of seriousness), I have observed that the sicker a patient is, the less likely they are to care whether or not their hospital gown is on correctly.

So in the continuum of healthy to sick, you have 1) the person that ties their gown on tightly and properly, then you have 2) the person that puts it on, but doesn't care in which direction, and finally, you have 3) the person who doesn't give a rats ass if their back (and other things) are exposed.

Obviously there are many other steps in between. Like the double gowner-- the person who puts one on in each direction-- my personal preference on a good day.

Therefore, how sick you are is inversely proportional to the degree in which you care about how wear your hospital gown.

Are you with me on this?

I have been at each end of the spectrum on this one. I remember what it was like to not care. I'd get out the hospital bed, and whoever was with me, be it my family or friends, would try to straighten me out, stuff me back into my gown, or re- tie it. I remember looking at them and laughing. I mean it's all so relative in the end. Now really: what does a hospital gown matter, when you can't breathe?

I bet anyone who works in a hospital could back me up on this (no pun intended)
-- Liz

<u>*Wednesday, May 15, 2002*</u>

Anxiety, anxiety, anxiety. This Saturday is the fundraiser "Turning Lemons into Lemonade" being held for my family and me.

Think about it. It is an event "in my honor", for which I am alive.

I don't mean that nearly as morbidly as it sounds. What I mean, is that once again, my bizarre life has given me a new type of experience to chew on.

And so I look forward with some trepidation…

It is so strange, and my feelings so ambivalent. On the one hand, I am extremely uncomfortable with the attention the illness has given me, but more humbly, I am just thrilled to receive the amazing energy others have to share. I know that it has been a tremendous resource, for all of us in my home~ in this dark time. I need to reframe the event in my own head, so that I can cope with the attention that my illness brings me, and appreciate all the goodness that there is. So, while it's a day that has come to be because of my Black Sea of bad luck, it's not about me. It's about much, much more. And I know I am blessed.

    -- Liz

<u>Thursday, May 16, 2002</u>

> *"Use your imagination not to scare yourself to death but to inspire yourself to life."*
> *-- ADELE BROOKMAN*

<u>Tuesday, May 21, 2002</u>

A reporter for the evening news aired our family's story recently. She asked me what I missed most about my old life.

I looked at her for seemed like an eternity (with a dumb look on my face) before answering that I didn't know.

What did I miss? It was such a loaded question...

When I thought about it, what did I miss?

I realized that while I miss so much, much of the things really don't matter and ultimately there wasn't anything I was actually "missing" except for one thing: the energy to enjoy life.

I now envy what most people take for granted: the energy that it takes to live each and every day.

I remember having some friends over, her daughter spilled her drink at the table. I watched as my friend, got up, went to the sink, wiped up the table and then got on her hands and knees to clean my entire kitchen floor in a few minutes.

Now don't get me wrong, my goal in life is not to clean (just ask my mother), and I really don't miss cleaning up after the kids all that much, but I was very envious of her right at that moment. That the task was so easy for her, and she didn't even know it.

Granted, this was also at a point in time where I did not bend over. I could not bend over. It would physically hurt my heart to do so. This time period lasted over a year; it's only recently that I have been able to bend over again. (Imagine what not bending over is like for a mother with two kids in sea of toys and debris. Yikes!)

At any rate, I have had this sensation before, once I was watching a young girl put on lipstick in the parking lot as she waited for a spot to open up so she could head into the movie theatre. I remember looking at her and thinking how she had so much and did not even know it (or maybe she did –what do I know?), and how she could look in her rear view mirror and just see lips that needed makeup.

And oh how I wished that I could just simply look in the mirror and see lips that needed some lipstick. That feeling, these thoughts, are what often remove me from the here and now, leading to this otherworldly feeling I get of existing in some type of surreal reality.

Anyway…the answer to the reporter's question? Energy.

-- Liz

<u>*Saturday, May 25, 2002*</u>

Yesterday was the 2-year anniversary of the day I became ill.

It is a strange day to commemorate, I know, but it gave me the chance to reflect.

I think back two years and I think how naïve I was when told that I had an incurable and progressive disease; and the difference between what I thought then, and what I think now.

I think about how I had (and still have) some romanticized notions about dying (I know, I know romance and death, can there be two words that are more dichotomous?)

Initially, I had this romantic notion about dying-- that the world would be a kind and gentle place where all of your final wishes came true…. as the world faded to black…

Wrong.

Instead I would suffer loss after loss, one more painful than the next. (And they haven't even stopped yet.) Every time I think that my life has hit bottom, I realize--OH! There's further to go… What I expected to look like a Hollywood or Hallmark movie ended up looking more like a really bad reality show for FOX.

Romantic Notion #6,789: *I would understand the purpose and meaning of my life; somehow it would all become clear.*

Wrong.

There was never that light bulb moment- where I suddenly understood my purpose in life. I didn't realize my life calling one morning, or wake up knowing what was missing from my life; quite conversely, I realized that I had all I ever needed. I wasn't missing or looking to change anything.

Romantic Notion #10,678: *You don't get to buy whatever you like...you don't miraculously get to live the Lifestyles of the Rich and Famous.*

So that trip to Europe that you couldn't afford before you got sick? Guess what: You still can't afford it. There is still the mortgage, the loans, the credit cards, etc.

When I finally came to terms with not caring about my personal debt, I started making whatever plans I cared to; I realized that all the wanting in the world couldn't help me travel, because by that time I was too sick to go anywhere. This was a bitter pill to swallow.

Made plans to go to Arizona, had to cancel; made plans to go to the Dominican Republic, where Scott and I eloped ten years ago (much to the dismay of our parents), had to cancel.

We did manage to squeak out a trip to Disney World with the girls even though I was confined to a wheelchair for the trip...

But going out of the country with Flolan is discouraged, and the thought of being "chained" down really bummed me out.

Soon I'd be told to stick to the Northeast, but I still kept busy, fantasizing where I might go – even though I really haven't gone anywhere. Soon though; soon, I console myself.

Romantic notion #17,889: *I would hug and kiss everyone goodbye as though it were my last time, every time. My relationships with my family and friends would be uncomplicated, simple, and "good to the last drop".*

Wrong again.

Relationships have become more rewarding, no doubt.

Most of my relationships have come through my illness unscathed. Many of them stronger, than before.

And while some have been damaged, most have been repairable, and have grown stronger because of the stark truths that life and death present. Most importantly, I learned that expectations are a pretty dangerous thing. I learned that if I was thinking what someone "should do", "shouldn't do", or "could do"; or if they thought I "should" or "shouldn't", or "could'" or "couldn't"-- that it was toxic, and a setup for disaster. I know now that people--including myself-- can only do what they can do, when they can do it; and to expect anything else is just a recipe for tragedy.

Only the one friendship was irreparable, lost for good. Lost is even much too passive a word, and doesn't adequately explain the end of that relationship. More to the point, it was the relationship that exploded and burnt us both in the end.

In the scheme of things, I guess that's a pretty good track record overall. So I am fortunate.

I learned that expectations can lead to big disappointment. And that is not as negative of a lesson as it sounds.

People can only do as much as they can at that given moment. Period. End of story.

Even in the never-ending disaster that my life feels like, with one bad thing after another... there is much good.

A few weeks ago I found something I wrote quite a long time ago entitled "how lucky I am"... I chuckled at the title before I even read the piece.

But I did read it; and as I did, I realized that while so much had changed, many of the feelings I wrote about then are the same now; I sighed a breath of relief as I realized – I could keep the title.

-- Liz

> "When we honestly ask ourselves which person in our lives means the most to us, we often find that it is those who, instead of giving much advice, solutions, or cures, have chosen rather to share our pain and touch our wounds with a gentle and tender hand. The friend who can be silent with us in a moment of despair or confusion, who can stay with us in an hour of grief and bereavement, who can tolerate not knowing, not curing, not healing and face with us the reality of our powerlessness, that is a friend who cares."
> -- Henri Nouwen "Out of Solitude"

How To Accept Help

⟋⟍

I know, easier said than done, on so many levels.

The first thing you will have to do is keep your circle of family and friends informed in whatever way is best *for you*. People worry about you, love you, and if you don't keep them "in the know", you will find yourself fielding telephone calls and emails non-stop. First, take a deep breath and accept all these calls as a blessing, not a nuisance. Take solace in it. It's nice that so many people care, but for your health's sake you will need to be proactive and control the amount of information you are willing to share. Some people are more private and some less (some days I announce what ails me in my Facebook status, other days I hold onto stuff and it more or less needs to be pried out of me). Do whatever is right FOR YOU--whether it's through a Caring Bridge personal website or regular emails, this will lessen the general anxiety around you and your illness. The bonus of course is that you won't be repeating yourself *ad nauseum*.

Many people will offer to help, and since most of us generally are used to functioning independently, we don't know how to accept this help. Maybe we are embarrassed, or even ashamed in some way. *Illness can dismantle us in ways we never thought possible.* Maybe we don't know how to ask for help, and I'm guessing that it's quite possibly even harder to accept help. If you find yourself in this predicament, accept the help.

People want to do anything they can to alleviate some of the burden that comes with illness. Again, take a deep breath and graciously accept. People will offer to help, but funnily enough, they won't know *how* to help you. You must--and this **critical**--*tell them what you want done*. If you don't, they will do things that they think are helpful, but in fact end up stressing you out.

For example, someone might offer to bring you to an appointment, when really you would prefer that they drive your children somewhere, or vice versa. Someone may bring food to you, when cooking is the only activity you are able to manage on your own.

Therefore, when people offer to help, guide them. This is going to feel awkward and alien at first, but it will help set up boundaries for people. This is extremely important for both parties, especially when you don't know if the help you need will be temporary (weeks or months) or become a way of life (years).

Here are some things people can help easily with: Pick up something at the grocery store or the drug store in order to save you a trip out. When someone stops by to see if you need anything, ask them to do something you have a hard time doing--things like, *Can you put this load of laundry in the wash? Can you bring up the load in the dryer? Can you bring the garbage to the curb?*

These are all relatively simple tasks that a seriously ill person would find impossible or near-impossible. The helper may think it's "nothing", but take it from me: Sometimes these "little things" are just what is needed. These "nothings" to you "normals" out there may seem small and inconsequential, but you have no idea of the enormity of the gift you have given, just by doing them, to someone who is bedridden or incapacitated.

Delegate whenever possible. I was very fortunate to have many people willing to help. My father-in-law was in charge of insurance and bills. As they came in, he sorted what was paid what wasn't, and kept on top of the billing departments. This was incredibly important and no small feat. Money worries are so stressful and damaging. Try to limit the time and energy you spend on it. Truly, you don't need to add to your worries. (I know some of you are laughing in disbelief right now, thinking that it is an impossible task, but please take my word for it. When I became ill and no longer worked, it meant we were surviving on just Scott's salary, which at that time was about $40,000 for a family of four.) It is possible to focus on other more important things. Commit yourself to your well-being. Freaking out and anxiety?—buh-bye. If you can find a family member or friend to trust with this insurance chore, hand it over willingly. You don't need to "know" any of this at this point in time. Again, let your # 1 focus be your health.

If you are waiting for a transplant, chances are you have been told you need to fundraise. I remember being incredibly stressed out with the whole thing initially. Again, if people offer to help, *let them*, and *delegate*. Let your friends start a fundraising committee, or a circle of support --whatever they want to call it. This is a time to let go of control (and control issues!) and NOT worry. I know easier said than done, but just trust that whatever needs to happen, will happen.

None of this will come easy. I can tell you this firsthand: Some things will be more challenging and some less so. Everyone is different.

If you are lucky enough to have people step up to the plate for you, you may feel overwhelmed with gratitude--don't let this stress you out either (also a lesson learned firsthand). Do what you can to express your gratitude (cards, letters) but again; don't let this become a chore that stresses you out more.

Give yourself permission to slack off on things that you would normally do (especially if you have children). Most importantly, forgive yourself for not being able to do all things at once.

If you don't have enough help and there are either not enough or no offers at all, reach out and ask! Seek out some help, whether through your community, church (churches often have teens that need volunteer hours), or many non-profit organizations. There are many groups and individuals who would love to help you *if they just knew how*.

Lastly, there are some chores and jobs you might be better off paying someone to do. I had a teenager come for a few hours a couple times a week, and I would just ask her to do things I couldn't do: Help me empty out drawers, sort through the kids' clothes that they had outgrown, take trips to the Salvation Army, get the Christmas decorations out of the attic, put them back in the attic, etc. By paying her, it freed me from having to ask my husband and children all the time. More importantly, it freed me from the guilt of always feeling like a constant burden (and pain in the ass). A win-win all around.

Now comes the next hard part. You may be surprised at who steps up to help. It may be close friends, family, or it may not. It may be your neighbor, an acquaintance or even a total stranger that steps up and helps. Realize now you never know where your angels will come from. And here comes the hard part about expectations: The "shoulda-coulda-woulda" part.

You may find yourself becoming angry with someone who you thought "would be" or "should be" helping you, and is not. Try not to be. People only can do what they can do. You will never know or understand the reasons why someone can or can't help you. Try not to get caught up in this. Don't get angry at them. Accept the help that is there for you and be grateful. You always have a choice: be mad at the person who wasn't there for you, or be grateful for those who are. Always choose gratitude, it's better for your health. I found out firsthand that I could be angry and hold a grudge at those who didn't help, but after talking with them I realized that I was partly responsible, because I didn't let them in enough for them to know how to help, and they ended up feeling that others were "taking care of it" and there was no room for them. This goes back to the beginning where I talk about being clear about what your needs are.

My honest guess is that at some point in time during your illness, you will feel abandoned by your family, friends and/or even God. If this desperation ever comes--and I sincerely hope it doesn't--communicate with those around you. Sometimes people back off to give you the space they think you need or because they don't know how to deal with you. They are afraid. Maybe they think you are just fine with things the way things are. In the same way that you are afraid of what the future may hold, they are afraid too. You may be the person who is ill, but remember, you are not the only one who is suffering.

How To Give Help

         ~ ᴄ

Sometimes all we need is someone to just listen and hold our hand. Other times we will need a "doer"--someone who sees what needs to be done and steps in. Parents at my girls' elementary school stepped right up and organized a dinner crusade, where meals were delivered 3 or more times a week for 2 years (maybe more), which was amazing and wonderful.

A couple of tips for helping with a food event like this:

1) Make sure you know what diet restrictions a person has, and bring the food over in containers that you don't need back. It's really hard to remember, mark and keep track of all those containers. Remember, you want to make things easier, not harder on people. Consider leaving a cooler by the front door or the side door, so meals can be left there; this way you don't have interrupt the sick person, and you can drop it off whenever it easiest for you. This also makes it also easy on the sick person, if they are out at a doctor's appointment or sleeping.

2) Use websites and emails to build a support network. Lotsa Helping Hands (www.lotsahelpinghands.com) is a great one that was not around when I was ill, but I have seen it work its magic.

For those wishing to help:

3) Ask what people would like help with, or offer something that you may see needs to be done. They can say "no" if they don't want you

to do it. I had a friend that would come over and visit and give my bathroom a quick clean up, that was incredibly helpful to me since bending over to clean the tub or toilet was pretty much impossible. I had another friend that came over before Christmas each year to help wrap Christmas gifts. I know, who would ever think a person would need help wrapping? But the activity left me out of breath-- cutting, wrapping, and taping. Ugh, too much.

4) If you are out of town and can't help with the day to day stuff, come over to visit. But please remember that you are there to help! Please make your own bed and your own food. Don't make things harder on the person you're visiting, I know that sounds harsh, but isn't it common sense? I was always very nervous about having people come over, and I feared that I would pressure myself into hosting and then I would be left more frazzled and exhausted. So as the visitor, do something with them they can't do on their own. Clean out a closet, organize something, paint--whatever they are comfortable with, and then leave. Um…I mean "don't over stay your welcome". One or two nights are usually sufficient.

5) Another great way to help if you are not in town is financially. My family is all out of town. They would all chip in on a monthly basis for someone to come clean the house, a much-appreciated gift.

6) Lastly ask yourself, *"Why I am helping?"* The answer is really important. There are good reasons to help, and believe or not, some not-so-good reasons. You should know before you step up what your intentions are. For example, are you helping for the sake of helping, or are you helping to satisfy some other need? By this I mean, are you helping to make yourself feel better about your- self? Are you helping in order to make yourself less guilty about some completely non- related incident? Or are you helping out in hopes for some kind of karmic tit-for-tat deal? These are really unhealthy reasons to help someone, and will usually end up hurt- ing both parties in the end. So before you volunteer to step up

and help someone, be clear about your intentions. It will ensure a strong healthy helping relationship for both parties.

<u>*Wednesday, May 29, 2002*</u>
I am tired and weary, the holiday weekend has passed, and I still have not received The Call. I am anxious to get The Call and have my transplants. I have been at the top of the list since the day I was listed. (Yes I am the only person waiting for a heart lung in my region with blood type B). Waiting has become very hard at times. This is one of those times.

You see, transplant centers are busy during holidays. That's the unfortunate reality of it all. With holidays come accidents, and donors.... And so while that sounds very morbid...it is a time of hope for me, when I think that maybe, just maybe... that magic call will come, and that it will be my turn.

So the weekend's over and I am still here, and it just makes me sad, other times it freaks me out. Like when I have trouble breathing, or my heart beats crazy and erratic, (not that either of these symptoms is unusual for me). More so, they serve as a troubling reminder to me that the clock is ticking and I can't help but ask myself.... will I get these transplants in time?

-- Liz

June, 2002

⁓

Tuesday, June 4, 2002

This past weekend was my daughter Luci's birthday. She turned 9.

She won't be able to say, "My mother died when I was 8."

Phew.

(Is there a psychiatrist in the house?)

Actually, five 9-year old girls slept over Friday night. They had busloads of fun. I got a baby-sitter.

Actually that's not true. We all had a great time. We did however get a baby-sitter the following evening, and went out to dinner at our favorite restaurant and to a movie…in lieu of the psychiatrist, I guess.

-- Liz

Wednesday, June 5, 2002

I used to go into the store and see clothes in size 0 and size 1 hanging on the sales rack, and I'd say to myself "Who the hell wears that size? No wonder it's on clearance, it couldn't possibly fit anyone…" Little did I know that there is a good part to being so small, and thin; I get to buy the sizes that no one else does.

Actually I no longer fit into 1's, I've moved into 2's in the past few months (which really says a lot about how small you really have to be to get into a 0.)

I fit into kid's sizes too. This works out great because kid's clothes are much cheaper than adult clothes…so I can go out to the girl's department and rack up. Often I do, buying the same thing in three different sizes- one for Emma, for Luci, and one for myself.

Hey- it keeps me entertained!

-- Liz

<u>*Wednesday, June 12, 2002*</u>
I have returned from falling off the face of the earth…

Actually the destination was Hershey Park. We took the kids there for a few days. I am still recouping from the fun.

One might wonder: How can a woman, who can't breathe very well, go spend a few days at an amusement park? Answer: With two VERY, VERY, (OK three) important items:

- *A wheelchair, to make it around the park.*
- *A husband to push the wheelchair, (and to go on the roller coaster rides with our fearless 9-year old.)*
- *And a rain poncho for the water rides, (yes a rain poncho) to cover my catheter site on my chest, since it can't get wet.*

So while everyone else is in their bikini tops and shorts in the sweltering sun, I am covered head to toe in plastic being pushed around in a wheelchair…. Needless to say I got a lot of strange looks, but it was a rip and definitely worth it.

I needed to get away, to go away…. I needed the self-inflicted break from reality.

Last week I found out that my hospital recently did a heart lung transplant. This is good and bad news. Let me explain…

It is good because it means that every time they do the procedure they get better at it…so that's good for me. It is bad, because I know that statistically the chances of receiving donors is pretty slim. On average, the center has maybe 1-2 heart lung transplants each year.

So I just watched one of my chances go "poof"…

I was very disappointed and very, very sad…hence the escape to the all-American pastime of thrills chills and spills….

I feel a little better now.

-- Liz

<u>*Friday, June 14, 2002*</u>
The search for healing has led to me to some pretty neat, obscure, and amazing places. I think if it's "out there" I have taken it, thought about taking it, tried it, eaten it, drank it, bathed in it or rubbed it all over my body.

I have learned that there are no hard and fast rules for anything in this lifetime, so I am willing to explore any options available to me in search of healing. I guess that is what happens when you are told you have an incurable and progressive disease. You learn pretty quickly, the hard way, that the science and medical arenas don't always have all the answers.

I have tried nutrition, supplements, homeopathy, acupuncture, herbs, Reiki, yoga, reflexology, massage, chiropractic, hypnosis, and visualization. While none of these activities have led me to THE miraculous cure, they have all been important, in their own ways, for their own reasons.

One practitioner has been indispensable. He is a healer, an energy healer and intuitive. While I cannot understand or even explain exactly what he does, I can say without a doubt he has been critical to my emotional and physical healing. "Amadeus" also taught me some important lessons that I needed to learn about joy, forgiveness, letting go, and most importantly, surrender.

I met him in April 2002. He is a 3 hour drive away in New Jersey. When my friend Jodi told me about him, more like gushed over him, I was in no position to make that trip physically because of my illness. I thanked her for the information and said I would likely not go, because I couldn't sit up for that length of time. The ascites in my belly, and the fact that I simply could not sit upright for that length of time, made it impossible for me to consider. Jodi put me in her car and drove me down. I laid in the back seat the whole ride there and back.

*The experience is very hard to describe. He does part energy work, part intuitive, part nutritionist, part therapy and healing. Although, all those words do not adequately describe the experience. His visits initially at least, always left me in tears and he was able to do what no doctor could, which is relieve my pain. Sometimes I would cry simply in disbelief, how could the pain be gone, so easily? Sometimes it would be immediate, other times I would still be in pain for the ride home only to get out of the car and then notice – **Hey the pain is gone!***

After my first visit there, I no longer needed to lay down for the ride, I could sit up and soon I could even help drive.

If you believe that our bodies are energy (and I do) then what he does is to realign the flow of the energy to make people well. Here is the best analogy I have for my experience with him. So imagine water flowing in a creek bed and a storm comes, it becomes misaligned, (sickness) he realigns the water and the flow of the creek (and you feel better) however, that creek bed still naturally goes back to the old pattern and it continues to need realignment again and again, till the new pattern is engraved and entrenched in the earth. That is the way it is with him. You go and the pain or the illness comes back- and each time you visit, the pain (illness) lessens, and the time between flare up lessens, until one day it is gone, and the new creek bed has been formed. Yes, the experience can feel miraculous.

Each healing experience has helped me learn something about myself, and something about my body. It's like climbing a ladder out of a very dark and deep pit--you climb slowly and deliberately, and you realize as you look back (and forward), that without the rung underneath you, you can't get to the next rung...

That's what this journey has been like for me. No one specific thing has been the "winning ticket", but I believe that every single "rung" has been completely necessary in order for me to get "there".

My friend and I went on a field trip of sorts the other day to visit an intuitive in Ithaca (of course, where else?).

Anyway, this woman has recently written a book where she talks about her journey into healing by way of music. Violins to be exact. She is a violin maker turned intuitive, who has learned to use her energy to not only tune violins, but to heal people. She does not read the future or anything like that. She says that she knows by admitting this to the general public, that the consensus may very well be that she is "a couple instruments short of a symphony".

But I guess that she is willing to take that chance. So we visited her in her healing center, a Frank Lloyd Wright Prairie-style home on the west side of Cayuga Lake. Very beautiful and peaceful.

Anyway, what brought us there was a specific chapter written in her book about transplant recipients. She believes that her healing energy can be infused into the donor and recipient's organs, thereby making the transplant more successful and reducing the chances of rejection.

After meeting her, I have decided that her official title is "Organ Cleanser"... (Little joke, get it violin? Organs? He, he, he).

Anyway, I am always impressed with people that can think outside the ol' reality box...

I have always been known as a gamer...you can always count me in.

-- Liz

<u>*Friday, June 21, 2002*</u>

There are two songs that get much of the airtime in my head these days.

Once in a Lifetime, by the Talking Heads is one of them. It gets big-time airplay. The more bizarre my life gets to, the more I hear it.

"…And you may ask yourself…Where does that highway go?

And you may ask yourself…How did I get here?"

The other soundtrack constantly running round my brain is, You Can't Always Get What You Want" by the Rolling Stones… for obvious reasons, but most importantly I can be found humming (and re-humming), that, "if you try sometimes well you just might find

You get what you need …"

-- Liz

<u>*Wednesday, June 26, 2002*</u>

Painful conversation #678:

It happened during "Pillow talk time". "Pillow talk time", can be defined as

1, the time of night when children, in an effort to stay up later than they are supposed to, decide to tell you everything about themselves and their day; and
2, the time when adults, in an effort to extract as much information as humanly possible from their children, ask lots of questions and listen.

We were talking about the transplant one night (as you can imagine we do with some regularity) when Emma said "I am scared"… When we talked more specifically, I came to realize that what she was really scared of was not the surgery, but me getting to Pittsburgh on the airplane. I was feeling a little relieved since this was something (I thought) I could say something about, to put her at ease…I told her that planes were generally safe and that very few crash, then even went into the bit about planes being safer than cars…. blah blah blah…. I was stupid enough to think that maybe I was consoling her fear until my other daughter, Luci, set me straight, "Mom. You don't get it Mom, Emma is scared that the plane is gonna crash, because someone is going to crash it, ON PURPOSE…. like into a building…." Then Luci turned to Emma and said "Don't worry Emma no one is going to crash Mom, it's a small plane with only one person on the plane, they would want a bigger plane, you know, with more people". (Like no duh, Mom)

I looked at Emma's face, the answer her sister had given seem to satisfy her. My face on the other hand, must have looked horrified, as I realized all that my children have to deal with....

Good God.

Do they have a chance at a normal healthy life between the messed up world they live in, and the messed up mom they live with?

-- Liz

Saturday, June 29, 2002

A friend of mine and I were once comparing hospital experiences. He lives out west, in a small town; I live in a small city, in upstate NY.

He was commenting on how the small size of their hospital was very comforting to him because he always knew he would have a private room to himself. Perhaps if I wasn't the "Professional Patient" that I have trained so diligently to become, I might have agreed with him.

Instead I thought about it, for a long time, because as a "Professional Patient" (or, "PP"), I have had my fair share of both private and shared rooms (depending on the reason for hospitalization).

So I chewed on it for a little while...

As I sat and chewed, I counted the roommates...1, 2, 3, 4, 5, 6... (probably more). And then at least as many times when I had a private room. Don't get me wrong. Private rooms definitely have their pros. Like when there are too many people visiting to fit in a regular room. Once, my family ended up having dinner catered into the hospital room because there were so many of us. (And yes it was delivered, with plates and silverware. After all; it is New York City). It was also nice because then I would have my own fridge for leftovers, snacks and drinks (my own personal hospitality center)....

The nurses always loved to visit my room, because there was always some yummy treat in store for them. When they came in to start their shift they would always want to know what was on the menu for the day. Japanese Chinese, Italian, Dominican. Yum yum... even when the sight of food did nothing for me, it was still fun.

Ah but I digress…as only food can make me do.

Not a chance, I decided. Each and every one of my roommates provided me a valuable life lesson no matter how kind or intolerable they were; I couldn't trade that in for privacy (or for a hospitality center, for that matter). The lessons learned were too valuable.

As I write, I realize it's too much to write about all at once. So here are some of my favorite roommates; for reasons both good and bad.

Agnes, an elderly woman on the Cardiac Care unit (where most people tend to be older, and I was, very often, the youngest patient on the floor).

June, another elderly woman also in the Cardiac Care unit, who died on me in the middle of the night. Now that's no way for a roommate to behave.

Shanice, a young woman in her twenties with cystic fibrosis.

Ethel, another woman in the, yes you guessed it, Cardiac Care Unit. She knew everything about everything (much to the chagrin of the doctors, the staff, the nurses and her roommate!)

I will follow with more elaborate details on each, I promise…

-- Liz

July, 2002

⟿

<u>Wednesday, July 3, 2002</u>

*T*rain of thought has derailed again...

Due to the inhuman heat, I have been unable to form a sentence on paper (or in my head for that matter). I have been walking around my house like a caged animal.

Yesterday the caged animal's mate went to Lowe's (in an effort to soothe the beast) and picked up an air conditioner.

Things are a little saner around here today; I have safely completed my metamorphosis back into a human being...

-- Liz

<u>Sunday, July 7, 2002</u>

Roommate Agnes:

She was in her late 80s, and obviously the matriarch of her family. Her husband came each day to see her, and had tremendous difficulty sitting in the chair because of his own ailing health. Day after day, hour after hour, he would sit there.

Her children, who were in their 60s, also came each day to visit. They took turns. It was obviously physically difficult on all of them.

Then her grandchildren would take turns, bringing in the great-grandchildren for short visits.

Unfortunately, she was also suffering from dementia and would forget most of what happened during the day. And when the day was done, and the visitors gone, she would start to have these episodes of dementia and anxiety about being *left alone and then would forget altogether who had come to see her that day. She would ask me if her husband came, I would reassure her that he had been there ALL day. She would comment that the doctor hadn't seen her that day; I would list the doctors she saw and procedures she had had for the day.*

She was afraid of the dark too, and that would add to her general anxiety, so she asked if we could leave a light on. She didn't like to close the shades, so she left those up as well. Lastly, she would ask me to leave the curtain open between us when we slept because she felt better seeing that I was there.

Then, when I could hear her snoring, I would get up, turn out the light, lower the shade and climb into bed. I was amazed at how many people she had around her at all times, and how I thought how very blessed she was, but not really...because no matter how many people were there, and no matter how many hours they spent with her, she would not remember it. What bitter irony, I thought; to always have people around and still think you are alone.

-- Liz

<u>*Wednesday, July 10, 2002*</u>
Roommate June:
Also an elderly woman. She was struggling with pulmonary hypertension, like me. She was alone when I came into the room and she was having very difficult time breathing. She was, for most of the day, busy coughing and hacking. She could not catch a breath to save her life (literally). In the middle of the night, she began to hallucinate as well.

I knew it wasn't a very good sign. I knew she was getting ready. Finally I heard her stop coughing and hacking.

Finally, the struggle ended, and all was quiet. I was thankful for the peace; mostly because I knew how she struggled to breathe but to come to terms with taking her last breath. I knew she was finally at peace...

I didn't however; expect to see her still in the room when I got up the next morning. Apparently they had not gotten around to taking her out of the room after she died. They had not taken her to wherever they put people in the hospital when they die, while they wait to be claimed. Almost like lost luggage only much, much more disturbing.

This was freaking out my nurse and my family, who were slightly dismayed by the fact that my roommate was uh –dead.

It really didn't bother me, mostly because I had heard her suffer and suffer hard the night before. I knew she was in a better place, and for that I was grateful. I walked past her all day long, back and forth, back and forth. I had my meals, and when visitors came I advised them in a whisper, a la The Wizard of Oz, to "pay no attention to the person behind the curtain"…

But what did bother me was her family showing up, much later, in fact after they actually took her away to that "mystery place".

Her family came into the room looking for her about 10 hours later; huffing and puffing and scattered, mumbling something about not being able to get to the hospital any earlier because the car broke down or something along those lines…

I guess that was what upset me so much, that she suffered for so long; it seemed to me like she deserved something a little more dignified in the end.

So my heart broke for that woman that day- not because she died (because I really believed she needed to and was ready), but because she died alone; and it seemed to me (not at that time anyway) that no one, not the staff or her own family had the time to say goodbye.

-- Liz

<u>Monday July 15, 2002</u>
Going to Scott's 20th high school reunion was really hard on me for lots of reasons. Why am I so upset?

Because chances are that I won't see my 20th high school reunion.

Because there were 5 people in Scott's class that died since high school. And because it was very hard to know that in all likelihood that will be my reality. I felt like Ebenezer Scrooge being shown his grim future.

There was a poster board with cut out pictures of the 5 classmates that said "In Memory Of", and I couldn't even bring myself to look at the pictures. Even out of respect from them, I couldn't do it. Too close to my reality for comfort.

Really the whole thing was much too depressing. It was too loud for my heart, too smoky for my lungs…. I wished I could enjoy people's company, since I know many of his classmates. I started dating Scott when we were in college.

I cried all the way home for all the things I have lost--again…. and all the things I will lose.

-- Liz

Wednesday, July 17, 2002

There is so much to talk about.

I struggle with what I can say and what I can't say. What do I write about? What is too much? What is too little?

There are many things I talk about very candidly, I think.

There are many things I can't talk about in this forum for whatever reason. Maybe it's too personal (I know, I know, that's hard to believe -something I actually might keep to myself???)

Some things I write about and share some things I write about and don't share. Many things don't make the final "cut and paste". Some things won't get written about at all.

But even when I feel uncertain about sharing particular events or stories, in cyberspace, I do write about it. As you can imagine, my journal has grown to astronomical proportions. OK, maybe not that big -but certainly more than I ever thought I would ever write in my lifetime. It is rapidly reaching the 100-page mark. In another lifetime, if someone ever told me I would ever write anything of that length I would have laughed and told them to quickly go get another cocktail.

But there are lots of topics that I don't touch, for various reasons. Like for instance you may have noticed that (for the most part) I don't say much about my doctors or the medical establishment in general. Perhaps this is because I, as a "Professional Patient, know what's truly in my own best interest. I know that for better or worse, these are the folks that are going to see to it that I live and survive this nasty little disease.

So, really the question becomes," Who is holding the sharp, shiny object otherwise known as a scalpel?"

Not me.

Any questions?

Hum, that could possibly be my motivation…so I do not mention the subtle forms of torture I have endured during my stays at the hospital.

Conversely, there are many positive aspects about all the medical personnel I have connected with. However, if I shared some of the oh-so-many-wonderful things and interactions that have occurred, some administrator, somewhere, would have a cow and fall off their fine leather office chair. Rather than risk any trouble, I keep it zipped.

Therefore, you won't hear wonderful stories about doctors that write off my bill because they know I can't pay it. You won't hear about the staff that fits me in to the doctor's schedule on an hour's notice (unheard of!) the doctors that stay at their office till 6pm so I can make the trip through Friday afternoon traffic in New York City, or the staff and doctors that save and give me samples of medicine that is otherwise outrageously expensive. The doctors who call me on Sunday to make sure I am ok. The doctor that comes to my house to drop off large boxes of medicine, or the doctor that offered to fly me to Pittsburgh. You won't hear about the nurse that comes to my house to check my breathing and heart rate because I feel too sick and tired to spend 5 hours in the emergency room, or the doctor that stopped by my house in an attempt unclog my hickman catheter. NO SIR you won't hear that from me…but you should.

That is one thing that I have learned for sure, from all the medical personnel that have crossed my path: There is much more to healing than just curing.

-- Liz

<u>*Friday, July 19, 2002*</u>
"Ailing Woman" is apparently my new title, given to me by my local newspaper in their headline, "Benefit for Ailing Woman". That's me, Ailing Woman…

My friends and family are getting a lot of mileage out of that one.

I may be sick and I may be frail, but "Ailing Woman" sounds, well…old.

It certainly does not describe me. I feel a little spunkier than that (I think!) these days. Most people when they see me say I look very good, for a person waiting for transplant. I'll take that as a compliment since I know what I looked like when I was really sick and frail.

Last week we went to the beach. This week we are taking the kids camping.

I am ecstatic that I have the energy to do it. I can't swim or get sun (and you may ask then what the point of the beach is). I can have fun…altered fun, but fun

nonetheless. *Someone once said "if it's worth doing, it's worth doing half-assed"…*
and that's how I feel right now. I'll take what I can get gladly and thankfully.
  -- Ailing Woman

<u>*Thursday, July 25, 2002*</u>
I read an article in today's paper about a doctor treating pulmonary hypertension with
Viagra. I was thrilled. There it was in the mainstream media. Perhaps it will become
an acceptable treatment soon! As I have mentioned before, I took Viagra for my PH for
a long time. Recently I stopped; it just seemed to stop working. The doctors think that at
some point, some of the other medicines I take must have rendered it ineffective.

  I started taking it in May 2001, on a wing and prayer, literally. "Compassionate
use" was the term they used (translation: we got nothing to lose). I was put inpatient
for about a week to monitor the medication, to make sure I would not drop dead
from a heart attack. The other term they used was "Experimental use"-- code word
for "not covered by insurance". In retrospect, the doctor confided to me that he had
said a prayer of thanks when I didn't drop dead from the treatment. Fortunately, I
could relate to his feeling at the time, because my sentiment was the same.

  I went through a great deal of emotional torture deciding whether or not to
try the drug. In the end, Viagra helped me breathe better for a long time. However,
it was very expensive.

  Surprise, surprise, Viagra is only covered for use by men. Isn't that insane,
their sexuality is covered, but my ability to breathe isn't?

  Now of course one could argue that the market is made up of males, so of
course logically they would be the people to be covered, but I think the marketing
is overlooking people like me. I could be a very good customer. Really. While there
may not be many of us, I make up for it in sheer numbers. Two pills every day, for
months or even years on end? That's probably more Viagra than a small suburban
neighborhood can consume.

  You should have seen the amount of Viagra cardboard packaging (sample size)
that left my house in the recycling bin. Imagining what the garbage men must
have thought when they picked it up made us crack up.

  I am glad to see that it is growing in acceptance (no pun intended); I abso-
lutely, positively, know it could be helpful to many people.

And the answer to your question is No; it didn't have any effect on my sexuality. Darn! Actually being off it has done more for me than being on it.
Go Figure :)
-- Liz

Viagra is now regularly prescribed to pulmonary hypertension patients under the name Sildenafil. See what I mean when I say things change quickly, and what is true today may not hold true tomorrow? HOPE.

My experience became part of the following research: Sulica R, Dinh H, Fuster V, and Poon M: "Beneficial Effect of Acute Sildenafil Administration in Pulmonary Hypertension secondary to Pulmonary Fibrosis" (editorial), Hurst's The Heart on line, October 2002.

August, 2002

Roommate Shanice:

She was a young woman in her early twenties, with cystic fibrosis.
She gabbed, gabbed, gabbed on the phone with friends while simultaneously watching very loud talk/reality shows, all day long. Probably not unlike most teenagers, I think.

Sometimes I'd ask her to turn the TV down.

The difference of course was that she wasn't dangling her legs off her bed in her own bedroom. It was a hospital. Over time, it became clear to me that the reason she looked comfortable and at home, because she was at home.

The hospital had become her home. She was spending months at a time fighting lung infections, and chatting and gossiping away on the phone with all her friends.

I realized these phone calls were her relationships.

Then after talking with her briefly, she explained to me that she had no real family other than a twin brother, who like her, also had cystic fibrosis. He had died about 4 months earlier.

I knew exactly why she had Jerry Springer turned up so loud. I think sometimes the noise on TV was preferable to the noise inside her own head. I could understand and relate to the feeling. I found myself a set of earplugs, and never asked her to turn the TV down again.

-- Liz

<u>*Tuesday, August 6, 2002*</u>
Roommate Ethel:
Now this woman knew it all, and was willing to share it. She was a woman in her fifties with some type of heart problem. She had something to say about everything. Advice for everyone. Complaints for everyone.

My understanding while staying in a hospital with a roommate is that when a person's curtain is drawn around them, generally they are resting. Open curtains, means open to conversation. I think that is how I have come to understand hospital etiquette, anyway.

Well, apparently Ethel did not know or did not care. She would talk, talk, talk non-stop. Complaining about the doctors, the nurses, the hospital, anybody and everybody on staff.

And she had advice about everything: Don't talk to anyone but your own doctors. And, don't let those interns or fellows work on you either, they don't know anything, they'll kill you. She'd say this mostly right to their faces as she kicked them out of the room.

She was the person that tells you, "Don't eat the chicken- I ate it yesterday…" while of course you are in the middle of eating the chicken. "I am telling you", she'd say, "that was the worst, driest chicken I ever had- it should be illegal for them to give us this crap…" Of course she would then add a description of the juicy tender chicken she makes at home to perfection.

Mostly I would just nod and smile. I watched as she quickly alienated the medical staff. Then I watched as her prophecy came true because no one was taking care of her, just as she predicted (surprise surprise). She would trash every single person that came in the room. They stayed away.

Finally one night, while all was peaceful and the curtain drawn she whispered to me "Does the right heart catheterization hurt?"

I told her she had nothing to worry about. While I hated the actual procedure, I had had it many times. I told her all about it, it would only hurt for a short time. She breathed a huge sigh of relief and went to bed.

Ah Ha! Now I understood. Inside that rabid Rottweiler was a scared little bunny.

The morning of the test, she was quiet and polite, as nice as could be.

After the test she went back to her rabid old self. But now I knew her little secret.

-- Liz

> *"You can stand tall without standing on someone.*
> *You can be a victor without having victims."*
> *-- HARRIET WOODS*

<u>*Saturday, August 10, 2002*</u>
Here is a copy of a letter I just sent to all my doctors, nurses and coordinators:

"To all my health care providers,

I just wanted to take a minute and let you all know that I am doing really, really well.

Thank you for all the support and wisdom you have given me these past two years.

As you all you know, I have been very sick for quite a long time.

I want you all to know that I could not have come this far without the help of each and every one of you. And while I know that there is no cure for Pulmonary Hypertension, I need you all to know that you have all shared the responsibility in my healing process.

So while I may never be 'cured', I am really doing quite well considering the shape I have been in. Thank you.

I haven't had a stomach tapping since January,

I haven't been hospitalized this year at all.

My quality of life has improved tremendously.

This summer I was able to vacation with my family at the beach (I could have never walked the distance to the water before or even taken the five hour car ride for that matter!)

I was also able to go camping. Yes, me and my two IV pumps roughed it for a couple of days (on an air mattress of course)

I am able to go to the basement in my house (if I feel like doing laundry) and to the second floor of my house where the girls' bedroom is. If you have children, you have an idea of what it looks like. So it's not a trip I take often by choice! But I can go up there if I need to.

My energy is good (not great), my breathing is good (not great), I exercise regularly, and I have gained almost twenty pounds! (I am probably the only person who could say that sentence joyfully).

Overall, I am more than okay.

And I am very thankful.

However feeling well brings questions and doubt.

So I bring the questions to you, all of you...

And while I know none of you have a crystal ball to see what the future may hold for me.... I know that there is some input that I could definitely use.

So with that, the first?

Can I try to wean off the Dobutamine? Has that been done? How is that done?

I realize that not being on the pump will take away my status on the heart lung list. But perhaps being on the Dobutamine for a year has given my heart a chance to heal? (My chest has stopped being 'barreled' like it was for some time- maybe my heart is fitting in there better?)

I like that idea of course, because I then think that if perhaps my heart has healed some, maybe I can have 'just' a lung transplant instead....

I fantasize about this of course since I know that lung transplants are much more prevalent and successful than the heart/ lung combo...

So bear with me while I fantasize...

Also should I (at any point) be considering adding Tracleer to the Flolan? Or any other drug...

(I have an appointment with Pittsburgh the end of august for re-eval).

Perhaps I am just entrenched in denial...I don't know. But I'd like to think that on some level my body can and is healing.

But I imagine that all of you have a better idea than me.

I look forward to your thoughts,

Sincerely,

Liz DeVivo, aka 'Ailing Woman'"

<u>*Sunday, August 11, 2002*</u>

> *"We heal each other all the time, and don't even realize that*
> *we're doing it. Healing comes out of a very simple human*
> *relationship - knowing your life matters to another person,*
> *and connecting to something larger and unseen."*
> *-- RACHEL NAOMI REMEN, M.D.*

<u>*Wednesday, August 14, 2002*</u>

Responses from my letter to the doctors? Not as positive or hopeful as I wish. But it never is. As I said before- having hope with an incurable, terminal disease is like watching a fish on the nature channel swim upstream in the raging water of Spring to lay its eggs. You shake your head and say, That ain't gonna happen. Thank goodness the fish doesn't know that we are all saying this, because he might just cash it in, too.

Regardless, the fish swims.

The general consensus among the providers was something along the lines of, "Glad you are feeling better, you look much better".

No one is interested in changing the course I am on, but they are willing to look at it. They have me taking a whole bunch of tests when I go in the next few weeks so that they can judge the situation better. They asked me also to have an echocardiogram done locally so I could bring results to Pittsburgh when I come. Basically, they think there is combination of things going on: 1)I have learned to cope and compensate with for the disease; and 2)that the medicine has done its job of masking the symptoms, not actually making anything go away, just covering it up well enough for me to cope.

Not that they "didn't want to take away my hope", but that generally with diseases, where there aren't any cures, they "don't want to give false hope."

Boy oh boy, do I hate realists.

Basically the answer was "stay on the path you're on, we don't want to change a thing."

Hum.

I bet no one tells the fish not to bother swimming upstream because the chances are astronomical, right? But you know that the fish still does, despite the insane odds. It even makes it sometimes.

-- Liz

Friday, August 16, 2002
Today I went to get my echocardiogram done. The technician has done at least a half-dozen of these tests on me so I know him and he knows my heart and me.

I told that it seemed like my heart was struggling less and that what I was looking for was any changes that might explain that.

He gave me the test and said, "Without looking at the last test you took I couldn't tell you exactly. But I think it doesn't look worse, or at least if it is worse, it is only by a little." What, do these guys all get together and take a class entitled "Hope: How Not to Give It? "

Damn.

Well, it is better than the last echo I had when he was training someone else to use the machine and said things like, "You can get a really good study from Liz because her heart is so (hesitation)…enlarged. You can see the details really well. The blood flow is so pronounced and the walls so thick you can really see the flow, and the back flow, which you can't in a (hesitation again)…typical patient." Fortunately, he didn't hurt my feelings as much as I could have let them been hurt.

He apologized for talking about me in front of me, I told him it was okay, it nothing I didn't already know. I know the right side of my heart is large and getting larger, that my heart is not normal and that it's only a matter time before the darn thing quits.

I get it. I get it. I get it.

-- Liz

Friday, August 23, 2002

> *"The fact that I can plant a seed and it becomes a flower, share a bit of knowledge and it becomes another's, smile at someone and receive a smile in return, are to me continual spiritual exercises."*
> *-- LEO BUSCAGLIA*

I think that this quote best explains how I continue to function. It explains the source of my faith, hope and strength: Others.

When I see, observe, or become the recipient of someone else's faith or strength. I am given all those things.

I wanted to share some of the most poignant and amazing words people have shared with me. I have asked the authors for their permission, they will be anonymous.

The following are all letters I received through mail or email, with people I otherwise would have never known if it weren't for my disease or the web site:

Liz,

I had to write you again to tell you about the conversation I had with my 9-year- old about you. We were sitting at the dinner table and I was telling my husband and kids about you (I have a twelve year old girl and nine year old son). My son looked at me and said, "Mom, can I give her my heart and lungs?" I told him that of course not, he needed them.

He said that was okay, that you really needed them, too. I said, "If you do that you would die." It was then that he said that was okay "because you don't need heart and lungs in heaven."

It was one of those moments that just makes you cry; from the mouths of babes...

I told him that we don't take one life to save another but that both his mom and dad are organ donors and that if by chance anything were to happen to us that our organs would then be used.

I guess I'm sharing this with you to let you know just how much people, even strangers, care and that your story has made a difference in a little boy's life. Because you have told your story, my son is little bit more compassionate, a little bit more loving.

<u>*Tuesday, August 27, 2002*</u>
Here's another story that also took my breath away; this one from a woman whose son was in a motorcycle accident:

Hello Liz,

Well, we can finally breathe easy at our place. Our son is finally out of the hospital. He was released last Friday; he was in a coma 20 days out of 29.

He started therapy right away and has been three times already. He is making slow progress, but it is at least in the right direction. We travel 3 times a week for the therapy and visits he has scheduled with three specialists to recheck his spleen, lungs, ribs, and arm. They said the ribs would take 3 months and the arm would take 1 year to reach its maximum potential. He should regain about 70% use of it.

But for a boy who had so many internal injuries and a shattered arm, he knows that he is lucky and that he was saved for a purpose. We don't know what, and it may not be known for years, but someday he will know. He is thinking of completely changing his major. He never thought he wanted to do anything in the medical field, but he is rethinking his direction in life.

Things like this will do that to you, as you well know. He has so much respect for what some of his doctors and nurses do on a daily basis. He is thinking in the line of therapy or radiology. So during his recovery time at home, I have helped him set up contacts with various places that offer a variety of degrees in that field and others in the medical line that he was interested in. It gives him a goal every day and something to look forward to.

Half of his success will be attitude toward it all.

I finally got a chance to read your journal of entries that have been made since his accident. I can only pray with you that a donor does come along while you are in this 'healthy' stage. (I use the term lightly.)

I have to tell you, that when the doctors told us we had 48 hours to know if he would make it, all sorts of feelings, as you can imagine, went through my head. One of them being that our son would be a donor.

With having a student who just received a heart here locally, and my new friendship with you, it has become a conscious thought of mine. I never thought that I would have to think about it, but there it was, right in front of us. Your picture crossed in front of my eyes as I thought of it.

I tell you this because of one of your recent journal entries that you just wrote. I know that my son's couldn't be used for you, but I did think *that it would be a way for us to have him live on and help someone that so desperately sitting and waiting. It is a strange feeling, and I know that your thoughts of receiving your 'gift' have mixed feelings as well.*

Have a good day and try to get out in the sun and feel its warmth. We all know that it doesn't happen too often around the southern tier. Talk to you later...

Friday, August 30, 2002

> *"You are only coming through in waves.*
> *Your lips move but I can't hear what you're saying...."*
> *-- PINK FLOYD*

I returned from Pittsburgh yesterday.

No wonderful or terrible news. Some tests, like my breathing tests, showed some improvement. Unfortunately, my heart has shown no improvement. So there will be no change in my medicines, or in the type of transplant, as I had hoped (and dreamed).

The doctor said he was thrilled to see me looking so well, and that truly he was astounded at the progress I have made. He pointed out that when he had met me last year, he didn't think I could have come this far. He now thinks that the transplant's chances for success are astounding. That is truly great news. He also said that my name had come up a few times, so he felt hopeful that a call could come soon for me, but that he did not think that my heart could recover from the damage already done.

I think my response was simply, "Damn it."

I guess I have had so much practice hearing bad news that I have become gracious at it. (I save the tears, sobbing and hissy fits for later, in the car, or at home.)

Like when I was told that I had fluid around my heart, and that it could possibly be a one-time crisis, or it could be that the scleroderma had evolved into pulmonary hypertension (evil disease extraordinaire). The chances of that, they said were slim since pulmonary hypertension usually progresses over decades, and statistically very few people have this complication.

Oops!

Then they said, "Even though it's incurable, there are options for treatment-- often calcium channel blockers are effective in lessening symptoms; and if they don't work, perhaps a 24-hour permanent IV medication that you can never be taken off of, might work."

Oops again.

Then they thought that the use of steroids could help the lung disease and the hacking cough that left me turning blue. If not, perhaps I needed to do more a more intensive trial of Cytoxan (chemo) for six months.

See Liz sitting in the cancer center. (I am sure by now you get the idea...)

And finally, when I was evaluated for transplant, part of the process was to decide whether one or two lungs would be sufficient. After evaluation, I was told I would need two lungs AND a heart.

I am pretty good at hearing the worst case scenario...and this trip was definitely **not** it.

-- Liz

September, 2002

〜

<u>Wednesday, September 4, 2002</u>

I am a double agent. I have two lives- the life I have, and the life I dream about having.

　(I guess that might be true for all of us though)

　-- Liz

<u>Thursday, September 5, 2002</u>

Yesterday my children went back to school. I love being with my children, but those last couple weeks of summer are truly brutal. So as you might imagine, I took a big deep breath-- phew--when they got on the bus. Then my neighbor and I did the happy dance. As the bus pulled away, she said, "We should probably wait until the bus is out of view, don't you think?"

　Anyone near me for the past couple of days has heard me singing and humming away. You know what song I am singing if you are the mother of school-aged children, I am sure.

　I am relieved and in need of some serious rest.

　So "double agent #1" was bummed that the last holiday weekend of the summer passed with no call for a transplant. "Double agent #2" was happy to have the holiday weekend pass, see the end of summer and begin the fall.

　-- Liz

<u>Tuesday, September 10, 2002</u>

I wasn't feeling so good yesterday. As the day passed, I felt worse and worse. I knew I was in trouble when I pulled the first corner of the blanket up to make the bed and that was all I could do. I had to sit down.

*As the day passed, I got more and more worried. I always start to wonder then worry. Then I start making the mental list --**When do I tell someone? When do I call the doctor? When do I call the ambulance?***

*I could feel the disease creeping up on me; I can actually feel it in my veins. In my circulation, in arms, legs, and head...it is a strange and troubling sensation. I get the creepy chills, like the feeling you get at the end of a scary movie when you realize that the nightmare is not over...it's just starting again. It's a very dark and fearful moment as I realize ...**It's Back**. Then I start to wonder whether it's back for an hour, a day, or a lifetime.*

*I got scared and went to bed and then...**poof**...I realized that my cord was loose and dripping. Just like that.*

I have this high-tech medicine that is delivered using technology that measures and delivers in nanograms. It can beep and tell me if the line is occluded, how much is left, how much has been given, and if the batteries are running low. It even says good morning and good evening.

Damn. You'd think by looking at my pumps that they could possibly have GPS technology, to tell me where I am positioned on the earth.

But it can't tell me if it's unplugged.

*Oops Liz, you're not dying, **you're just unplugged!***

-- Liz

<u>*Wednesday, September 11, 2002*</u>

Last year, after I watched the towers crumble on TV, I called my friend at the time, crying, and simply said, "This Is a world filled with Very, Very bad people. How can we live in such a place where this is how people treat one another?" Ironically enough I said that to my friend who at the time was having an affair with my husband, little did I know I was speaking to the same type of person I was speaking about. Gratefully, I am able to look back a year later and know that what I said at the time does not hold true. My own personal experience tells me there is so much that is good, even within the bad. And while people can be evil, ultimately there are many, many other people who are good, warm, and full of love to share.

Through all the grief and loss, more importantly, comes hope. I'll cling to that.

-- Liz

Friday, September 13, 2002
Next Saturday, September 21, there will be a fundraiser in the NYC area.

Friends who I grew up with in Woodside, Queens have made all the arrangements. It will be a reunion / fundraiser. My family will be there too; even my father will fly in from Colombia, South America to be there.

I am really looking forward to it. I get to see the kids that I grew up with, all together, in one place! That is quite the task. When you grow up in the city, you can be neighbors all your life, and never go to the same elementary school, high school, after school programs, summer camps or church. So the typical "links" between people are missing-- it is definitely quite the effort. I am very much looking forward to (even if I do have that streak of tentativeness that shudders at the reason for) the party.

I am fortunate because in that crazy way (again) this disease has given me a gift: friends, reaching out from all nooks and crannies of my life. Most people don't get to see everyone they've ever cared about in their life. I am lucky--I do. (And I am even alive when it happens!) Double Bonus!
-- Liz

Sunday, September 15, 2002
Candy of the Week: Gobstoppers
-- Liz

Tuesday, September 17, 2002
Once I was in sitting in church, anxious and distracted. (OK, OK I admit, many times), but I am referencing one time in particular.

Anxious and distraught can sometimes be a normal state of affairs for me, as one might imagine. These are the raw emotions that have the power and ability to throw me over the edge. I went to Mass in hope of finding some peace and quiet in my head.

But as I sat there, I found that I was too distracted. I could not focus; I kept going back to the anxiety, the worry, and the wheels turning inside my head. I was becoming frustrated.

I asked God for help, to help me focus and to be present in the church and to help me focus my spirituality in a good and positive way. I knew I needed to get over the anxiety, and I was begging for some assistance from God at this point. I sat in the pew with my head in my hands. In the background I could hear the priest talking, I could hear words, words, words sounding much like the adults in Charlie Brown-- blah blah blah; then all of a sudden I heard "Blah blah blah…. Liz DeVivo."

I looked up. Direct hit. When the priest starts saying your name from the altar, you pay close attention.

He said some kind things about me and then asked the people in church to join him in a prayer for my health.

I was present, loud, clear, and accounted for. Very much so.

Apparently I (like Moses) need a burning bush, to get the picture.

-- Liz

Find somewhere that brings you peace. A physical place that helps you mentally and spiritually to find peace. Realize no matter what the outcome of your illness, whether you live or die, the ultimate goal is the same: to be at peace with your life as you know it, today.

We are all dying from the day we are born; each day, we are one day closer to our death. We just don't think about this reality on a daily basis until we are confronted with our mortality in the face of old age, an accident, or illness.

Please notice that it is not life **or** death. We don't get to choose. Inevitably, one just follows the other, it's just a matter of when; it's part of the life cycle. And regardless of when it comes or how, our "goal"--for lack of better or word--or the direction for our soul should always be towards the direction of peace. Our focus should be on the spiritual business we must attend to, in order to reach this peace.

Most of us go about our life blissfully unaware of our own death, rarely considering it until something like illness forces us to look.

We may not have a choice about dying, but we do have some choices when it comes to living and considering our own death.

If our intent is to live we may not even want to consider death an option--that is one choice. We can go about our life like living is the only option we are considering. We can also choose to hope for the best and prepare for the worst, a very pragmatic choice.

However you decide to prepare for or "frame" your own death is up to you. But it is the work that has to be done, one way or another.

As a mother of two young girls, I had some work to do to prepare for my death if not for myself, then for their sake.

Scott was not a willing participant in any conversation involving my impending death, whether he was in denial or eternally optimistic, the outcome was the same. He would simply reply, "Liz that's not going to happen..."

At the beginning of my illness when I was entrenched in illness 24/7, I could not envision any other ending to my suffering, so the concrete items were attended to: my will, my health care proxy-- legal matters were sorted and put away. Those were relatively easy matters. I thought about my wake, my funeral, and my obituary. While some people like to have a say in their services, and even write their own obituaries, I felt that the life I had led said enough about me as person; and that when the time came, those left could make the decisions on how to best celebrate my life. I think the only thing I actually did for my funeral at that time was to make a playlist. Yup, a playlist. I couldn't even bring myself to burn the actual CD; I just made a playlist of songs I would like people to hear when I die. That was it. Some of the songs: Many Rivers to Cross by Jimmy Cliff, Peace of mind by Neil Young, Seasons of Love from Rent, Beautiful day by U2, I Will Remember You by Sarah McLachlan, Blackbird by The Beatles.

I figured the rest was out of my control and jurisdiction, and I was better off that way; that I would be in a better place and they could and would do whatever they needed to do.

There is only so much one brain can think about on any given day, and my reality was pretty much consumed with "what ifs" for my girls.

So I did not fret that part. But there was plenty to fret about. I made books for the girls about me--who I was as a child, a teen, and adult in case they never got to know me. I taped their bedtime stories for them to hear, as well as stories about myself as a kid (they loved to hear me tell stories about me as kid as part of their bedtime ritual.)

I thought about a video, but the reality was I so frail and disfigured at that point, that this was not the way I wanted to be remembered. But I wrote lists of music and books I loved, in hopes that one day they could love them, too. Next, I found someone who is comfortable talking to me about death--specifically, my death. Not too many people are, but you will find them, and they may or may not be the people you expect. I had a few friends that would go there with me. My husband was not one with whom to talk about death. He was very good at other things, and excelled in the matters of our children and our home. But since he couldn't talk about the very real possibility of me dying, I just wrote in a spiral notebook all the things for Scott to think about saying to the girls when they had problems and questions as they moved to thru childhood to adolescence, and into adulthood. I called it my honey-do list from the grave, a "How To" manual of sorts, for a single father of two girls. It wasn't that I thought he couldn't handle it. It was that I wanted to ensure a piece of me would be present in their future.

I wrote about what to do and say when the girls had problems with friends, how to help them through their grief with me, how to not minimize their pain, to help them cry if they needed to, especially since I know how uncomfortable Scott is with emotions and feelings (he grew up in a household of boys!) I wrote about how to handle their first period, their first boyfriend, first heartache... I thanked him for being a good dad.

"Please don't replace me as you would a pet. Let the children (and yourself) be sad, feel sad. If they feel good and happy, then that's ok too. I get nervous that in your desire to not have them be in pain and feel the loss of their mother, they will keep it in – for your sake- to not rock your boat. I know that you don't know what to do with feelings that are uncomfortable (anger and sadness). Know that all they or anyone needs is for you to sit with their feelings, to just say it's ok to feel sad/ mad/confused/frightened, whatever. No solution necessary. Just love and listening."

I wrote in fear of never reaching those milestones with my children.

I prepared myself to die, and then I went about my life expecting to live.

Or as my favorite priest used to tell me, "Liz, don't ask for a miracle. *Expect a miracle.*"

Friday, September 20, 2002
My mother has her own way of assessing my health. It's different than the doctors' way, but just as valuable. Let me explain. When she calls me, she knows immediately from the sound of my voice how I am doing-- and she'll instantly scold, "You've been doing too much, I can tell. You want to do things because you feel better, but you don't realize you're doing too much." Or, "What are trying to do, hurt yourself? You know you can't be doing as much as you want to. Those girls need you. What do want to do--end up back in the hospital?" (No one could ever accuse my mother of not telling it like it is.)

After I am scolded, and I feel like I have made a return trip to adolescence. "I know Mom, you're right Mom." I say these things reluctantly, because I know that she is right. (Damn!) And because bottom line--nobody knows like a mother does. I know that now, and hope my own girls don't take forever to understand and receive their mother's love.

This summer my mother came to visit. She lives in New York City, , which is about 3 hours away; and while we try to see each other at least once a month either here or there, it has been tough since I have been ill, and hard to keep this schedule.

Not unlike most mothers, my Mom walks around my house and takes it all in. As I said, it is her way of assessing the situation.

First thing she said to me when she got out of the car was, "Your hair is shiny and curly." Later, she said to me in that tone of voice that only mothers have, "You seem to be walking with a little more energy." This was followed by questions regarding my weight and eating habits: "How much do you weigh now? You look like you are having no problem eating; you're filling out your pants" which to me are all compliments. I am the only person on earth who can be told, "Hey, you look a little chunky" and I would smile and kiss the person. Most people would get a slap to the back of the head. The other day my husband had a comment about the size of my rear. In another time and place, he would have gotten the evil eye. Instead he got a warm smile.

Anyway…. there is a running commentary while she walks around my house, as I imagine so many other mothers do: "Your plants are growing." (They haven't grown in a long time, because they were on the bottom of the list for a very long time. They were lucky if I spit on them as I walked by. Now they are healthy green and growing.) I had an orchid that was given to me as a gift. I basically killed it, but there was the slightest tiny bit of life left in it. I have nurtured it, and finally the plant has about 4inches of new growth. For me, it has become a metaphor for my life.

Anyway, I'll take my Mom's assessment over the doctors'. Any day.
-- Liz

Tuesday, September 24, 2002
I had so much fun; I have been in my pajamas for 2 days. Now that's a good party.

The fundraiser/ reunion was like an absurd twist of the Twilight Zone meets This Is Your Life or funeral calling hours.

I can't remember the last time I had that much fun. Saturday's fundraiser was of course, a great success. More importantly, it was really special, and it touched my heart and soul.

I can't remember the last time I laughed for about 6 hours straight. I was reminded by my friends, from childhood to adolescence; of many things I had long-since forgotten--probably on purpose. What we did, what we didn't do. The games we played, what we were supposed to play, where we went and where we were supposed to go. The more I talked with people and remembered, the more I realized the trouble I will be in with my own girls if what goes around comes around.

Uh-oh.

The kids I played with, the kids I dreamed with and shared my secrets with; the kids I got in trouble with and into trouble with, fought with and cried with. The kids we played spin the bottle with and then as we got older, dated. And now to have our spouses and children meet was just too, too wonderful.

What a great reminder of that magical time. It was the sweetest day I can remember having in a very long time.

"Believe in Second Chances"-- that's what the t-shirts for all of our fundraisers have embroidered on them. Being reminded of that magical time is a "Second Chance" to reconnect with everyone, and to enjoy it all over again.

-- Liz

<u>*Thursday, September 26, 2002*</u>
I step out of the shower and looked at my naked body in the mirror. I have a three-inch scar under my breast from the heart surgery. That is nothing, I think; the real scar will come someday soon (I hope). It will be large; it's called the "clamshell incision" if that gives an idea of the magnitude. It will go from one armpit, across to the other, under my chest.

I could freak out about it. I choose not to.

My guess is that one day I will be walking around showing off my scar to everyone I know, much like the kid who turns their eyelids inside-out and sends everyone running out of the room. Not that I'd really know. I have many talents--turning my eyelids inside out is not one of them.

All over my body there all kinds of other little scars; they tell a story.

I have scars on my neck from the all the heart catheterizations. I have little itty-bitty scars, more like dots all over my belly from the 16-plus (I lost track) belly taps. When I touch them, it's like Braille on my stomach; I can't help but wonder what the message is. It is probably something like "feed the chickens" or something obscure like that. On my belly there is one darker scar--more like a discoloration--the size of a quarter, which was from the last tap. It was as if my body was sending me a message: Here's the last one- and don't you ever forget it! I look at the discolored patch on my belly; I will never forget it. My body won't let me.

Those little bumps also appear on my chest were they stuck that stinking needle into my heart 3 times. (Can you say "PTSD"?)

I look at my body; overall I can say I have come a long way. I know I have come a long way.

My body was thin, gray, frail, and disproportioned. My chest was barreled--this is when the rib cage actually stretches to accommodate the enlarged heart and the fluid in the abdomen. I could feel my rib cage expanding, and it would hurt so bad sometimes it would keep me up in the middle of the night, crying.

Now my body is still thin, but not sickeningly so. I don't look or feel as frail; my coloring is pink and I am correctly-proportioned once again. This, in and of itself is a miracle, because I never thought I would see that day again. I threw away or gave away all my clothes to friends because I didn't think I'd ever wear them again.

A nurse once said to me, "Liz, are you ready to take on the battle of your lifetime, with these transplants?"

I said "Are you kidding? This is not a battle. This is the light at the end of the tunnel."

I am not fighting a battle; I am leaving one behind.

That's my plan anyway. That's how I choose to frame this event. It's the only way I know how without going off the deep end.

-- Liz

Friday, September 27, 2002

My beeper went off today.

It was a wrong number. I was taking a nap when it went off. Needless to say, I am not sleeping now.

It is the first time it has ever gone off.

The blood flow is just returning. Can I get some vitals over here?

-- Liz

Monday, September 30, 2002

"The very least you can do in your life is to figure out what you hope for. And the most you can do is live inside that hope."

-- BARBARA KINGSOLVER

October, 2002

_S_ome of my peers are people like me who are ill. They are people that I have connected with by Internet or support group, because we either see the same doctors, or because we have the same treatment. I see them suffer through these diseases. I also see them triumph. Either way, it's good to know that I am not alone.

Last week another peer of mine died. It is very stressful when your peer group is suffering so intensely that they are literally dying. On the one hand, they are a source of familiarity, comfort, and hope; on the other there is fear of what the future might bring.

This past month has been hard; three people have died either from their PH or from their transplants. It's tragic, quite disheartening, and very, very sad.

For instance, when I was just about to begin using Flolan, I met a young woman in the hospital--a single mom of a 2-year old, who was 28 years old and had just been hooked up to Flolan. She seemed to be doing well. A few weeks later she died.

Later when I was in Pittsburgh at the family house, I met a man who recognized my medicine bags and told me his wife had the same bags. She just recently had a heart-lung transplant, and was at the hospital. He took me over to meet her. She was about 32 and also had a child. She expected to be discharged that week; she also died.

Then there was the woman who was the on top of the list with blood type 'B' in her region (like me), and got called for her double lung transplant (unlike me). She died too. (Unlike me, I hope.)

It's very disheartening to watch what happens to people, and know that it, too, can be my future. I know the odds are not in my favor and that really the numbers are not very pretty to look at, at all.

A woman I talked to recently was on the list for over a year before being taken off for becoming too sick to transplant. Another person I know missed her transplant because she couldn't get there in time, the roads were flooded because of heavy rain, and no planes were flying. How in the hell do you deal with that?

There is a friend of mine, Allison who is in Canada waiting for a double lung transplant. We met through the computer, and have gone through much of this process together online. We joke about living parallel lives. She is the same age as me, with two young boys that are the same ages as my girls. Like me, she worked in the mental health profession before becoming ill. Much of the time our fears, dreams, and hope mirror each other's. We are comrades.

Anyway, when she was listed, she was told that she was 19th on the list.

We have watched her climb the list and now she is about 6th on list; we both know her time is coming soon. Strangely enough, I measure time passing by watching her climb her list.

I acknowledge and comfort myself--as I have so many times before--that SOMEONE is in control.... it's just not me.

-- Liz

Saturday, October 5, 2002

> "Verbs, all of them tiring."
> -- CHARLES FRAZIER

Saturday, October 5, 2002
Candy of the week: Altoids Tangerine Sours
-- Liz

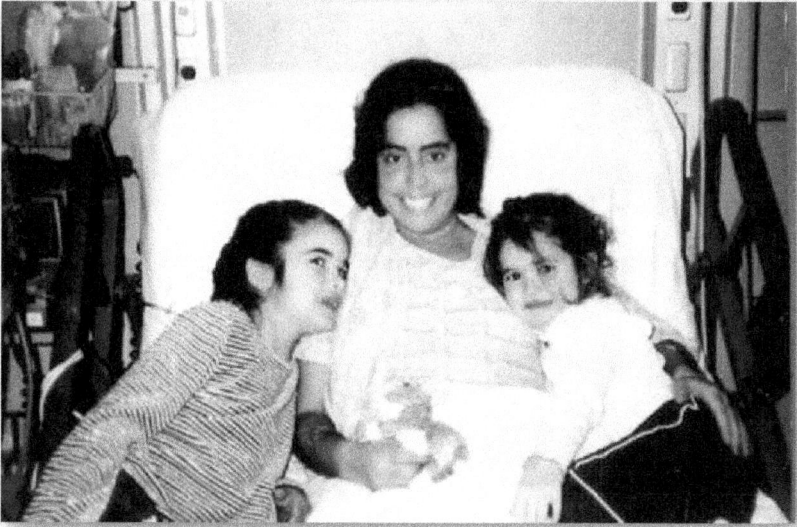

My girls and me, during one of my many hospitalizations. *Circa* 2001.

One of our many angel flights, this one from Teterboro Airport,
New Jersey…yes, it really was a pink airplane.

My mom and me, on the Angel Flight.

<u>Wednesday, October 9, 2002</u>
I wrote this a year ago for a Pulmonary Hypertension Newsletter published through the Pulmonary Hypertension Association around November of 2001. I reread it recently, and thought I'd share it here:

An Early Christmas Gift
By Liz DeVivo

I came to UPMC in August of this year for a lung transplant evaluation. I came from Binghamton, NY a 6-7 hour drive, which is a long trip depending of course on speed and stops.

It's a very long and tough trip when you are ill with PH, and it's little tougher when you are sporting symptoms of heart failure such as ascites. Scott and I decided to fly. It would be easier on my body.

When we left, our plane ended up being delayed about 6 hours. It was very painful for me to sit. Every couple of hours, they would announce further delays, some people would mutter or curse under their breath. I eventually just began to cry. I couldn't take the pressure of sitting, and needed to lie down. The trip was very hard on me. Eventually I found a chapel in the airport. I lay in the pew, asking God not to think me rude, I simply could no longer be upright.

We managed to get there, and spent the week in evaluation. One of the suggestions that came from that evaluation included returning to have a feeding tube placed and to start a dobutamine IV. I was unsure of whether or not I could start the treatments--I was unsure of how I would make the trip. It was after the tragic events of September 11, and I wasn't particularly excited about getting on a commercial plane again.

Time passed, and I finally decided that the treatment I had been offered could offer me hope. I committed myself to going. Now I just had to figure out how to get there.

I am married and have two young daughters, (5 and 8). Scott could not take me; we had agreed (after my many hospitalizations in the past year) that it would be best for him to stay home with the girls.

My mother agreed to come with me, but she does not drive. I had to come to terms with the drive on my own. I was scared, but definitely willing to do it, I had made up my mind that somehow, I would get to Pittsburgh. I reasoned and rationalized with myself, and said to myself, "You can stop as much as you need to"…. I was not looking forward to it.

Two days before we left, I came across a website that someone had suggested before, Volunteer Pilots Association. I emailed them and various other "angel flight" -type operations. I figured, what did I have to lose by asking?

Within an hour, Kevin, who heads up the Volunteer Pilots Association (VPA) had replied to my email. He thought he could help me. I printed forms needed off the computer; signed them and had them faxed the doctors in Pittsburgh. In less than 24 hours, he managed to secure me a volunteer pilot, and a plane that would pick up my mother and me and take us to Pittsburgh. I cried. I couldn't believe it. In the land of bad luck (which is where I generally reside with pulmonary hypertension), I was given this gift.

The plane was to pick us up in Teterboro, NJ, which has a small private airport outside New York City. I was told to expect a 4-person, pink-- yes, I said pink--plane. The volunteer pilot was a woman who owned a pink plane. I smiled.

When we arrived to the airport, we were told that because of the 9/11 memorial service at Yankee stadium there was a "no-fly zone" currently in effect. No planes could land or take off within a 50-mile radius. My heart dropped; maybe I wasn't meant to go.

Within minutes of being told we were going nowhere, I saw the pink plane land outside on the strip. Then, we were told we would be given clearance to leave because it was an Angel Flight. I felt strange and blessed as we took off in the very pink plane, knowing that we were the only plane in the sky for miles around.

A very aptly named Angel Flight, I thought.

Not only did the VPA arrange for us to get to Pittsburgh, but they also arranged ground transportation when we arrived at Allegheny Airport, dropping us off in front of the family house. Kevin helped us get home too, and then made the arrangements for my follow-up appointment the next month. My family and I were and are still in disbelief at the kindness, the unselfishness, and the giving we had witnessed with Kevin and his organization.

What happened to me that day was more than a gift-- it was a blessing. Divine Intervention some might think. I know so.

The next time I am scheduled to visit Pittsburgh is In April, unless of course I receive the call for my heart and lung transplant. Either way, I know the VPA will be there for my family and me, and that makes me smile.

-- Liz

<u>*Friday, October 11, 2002*</u>
Another good one from Barbara Kingsolver:

"People's dreams are made out of what they do all day. The same way a dog that runs after rabbits will dream of rabbits. It's what you do that makes your soul, not the other way around."

-- Liz

<u>*Tuesday, October 15, 2002*</u>
People say, "Liz you look great, you wouldn't even know to look at you that you are sick". Ahh.... but this was not always the case. I have heard it so often that I am actually starting to believe it. I see the look on people's faces that haven't seen me in year. Their look (that is one part happiness and one part relief) tells me everything I need to know. I can pass.

Do you know what a gift and privilege it is to be able to 'pass' as normal? (Even if only on the outside?) To be able to participate in reality, and not just hover around it, wishing?

Lesson of the day for Liz:
Never *underestimate the honor of status quo.*
-- Liz

<u>*Friday, October 18, 2002*</u>
Today, I am 36 years old.

Another milestone. Not that I didn't expect to see it, it's just that I would never just make that assumption.

So for right now, today, it's time to celebrate. I love my birthday, and I always have loved sharing it with friends and family.

Once while discussing my prognosis, my doctor shrugged his shoulders and said, "Liz, it's like Star Trek. You're going where no man has gone before."

Basically, he was saying there are no answers, guesses, guidelines, or guarantees. It is just what it is. It's no different for me, than it is for anyone else.

-- Liz

<u>*Wednesday, October 23, 2002*</u>

I never got to enter my post for Sunday, October 20th because I ended up in the hospital again...more about that after. First, the good news

OK. So I thought I was getting picked up to go out with my girlfriends, to have some dinner for my birthday. Instead, I ended up on the top floor of the State Office building here in Binghamton (on the eighteenth floor of the tallest building in this city anyway) with many friends, delicious food, and a balloon ñ in the shape of two lungs and a heart, that I beat the piss out of while my friends watched and cheered me on.

Scott threw me a surprise party. A wonderful, marvelous, excruciatingly fun, surprise party. He planned every detail and cooked the delectable food for it as well.

I was not only surprised. I was shocked. My husband thought I was going to pass out. In fact, I was so surprised I didn't even understand that it was my party- even when I entered the room. Talk about clueless.

It didn't happen easily either; I definitely put up some resistance. When my mother-in-law offered to take me shopping for a new outfit for my birthday, I declined saying I didn't need anything. "What do I need a pretty outfit for?--I don't go anywhere or do anything." She made me pick out something anyway.

When my father-in-law came to pick up my children, I told him. "No they can stay awhile longer we are in no rush." He took them anyway.

When my friend Beth offered to drive me to "the restaurant" this being the guise they worked under to get me to my own party, I said that I thought I should drive myself, because this way if I became tired, I could take myself home. She picked me up anyway.

On the way to "the restaurant", Beth mentioned that she was doing some work in the State Office building and wanted us to look at the space and see what she could do to decorate it for a future event. I said I didn't want to go, (too far to get out, park, and go into the building, I rationalized) I'd stay in the car. Six women in a minivan insisted that I get up and out, to check out the building.

The final straw was when we were parking the car. We passed Scott's car at the receiving docks. I said, "What is Scott doing here?" Everyone in the car said,

"That's not Scott's car." I hollered, "I know my husband's car!" Then, I tried to reach him by phone to see what he was doing.

Fortunately, the security man in the building, who insisted we all show ID and sign in, sidetracked me.

When we went up and saw the room, I saw that there was a party going on and thought that we were intruding upon someone else's party. It was only then understood what happened.

If I could have hit the floor without staying there permanently, I would have...

Instead I beat a piñata in the shape of my internal organs

My friend made it for me. A balloon sculpture complete with beating stick. We had been talking about what I wanted to do for my birthday this year. I told her I had no plans, but that I wanted to create a papier-mâché heart and lungs and then have some kind of festive public type of lynching ceremony with friends. A weird kind of "going away party", I guess.

Along with the balloon creation came directions for papier-mâché.

I have a sneaking suspicion I know what I'll be doing this week.

-- Liz

Instead...

<u>Wednesday, October 23, 2002</u>
I spent the last three days in the Cardiac Care Unit at the hospital.

I am tired and cranky.

It seems like the motto of my life is "Suck it up, Liz". I am so tired and sick of being sick--I can't stand it.

Obviously, I had no idea what I was going to be doing this week. I didn't think it would be this.

I had gone to sleep Sunday, exhausted from the birthday festivities, with visions of sugarplums dancing in my head. My pump and catheter had a different agenda. I turned the light off and snuggled into my bed, and as I did, the pump alarm went off. It was like some kind of sick joke, I would turn the light off, and the pump alarm would go off. I would turn the light on and then it would stop.

We played with the pump, tried to fix it, changed it over to the backup pump, and nothing. The cruel joke just continued. After calling the Flolan Hotline (yes there is such a thing,) we went to the emergency room. My Hickman catheter was blocked. They poked some new holes in my arm to hook up the medicines (remember they can never stop running) they did what they could to unblock it. In the end, they decided to replace it.

Three days later, I have new line, multiple stitches, at least a dozen holes in my two arms, and new scar to watch heal on my chest.

Now I realize that having to install a new line should have had a place all along on my "top-ten fear list". My hopes were that they would just pull out the line when I had the transplant. I hadn't even entertained the thought of them having to pierce a new hole in my body. Not me, I hadn't even considered the possibility.

Silly me. I never had a problem with my line before, nor any of the infections that other people commonly have--so I thought I was safe.

To add insult to injury, they put my new line in so that it now hangs down between my breasts. It used to run down along the side of my body. Very Awkward. Very Uncomfortable. The Doctor explained all the very rational reasons for choosing to do this; and while I couldn't be mad at him, I am disgusted and crabby.

It's like a new haircut on the first day; you look in the mirror and cry. Then you get over it.

Suck it up, Liz*.*
-- Liz

<u>*Friday, October 25, 2002*</u>

> *"Oh I used to be disgusted*
> *And now I try to be amused.*
> *But since their wings have got rusted,*
> *You know, the angels wanna wear my red shoes..."*
> *-- ELVIS COSTELLO, OF COURSE*

Finally...I had been holding onto that quote forever looking for the right time.
I think that this is the week for it.
-- Liz

<u>*Wednesday, October 30, 2002*</u>
Staying at the institution of care (and torture) that we call a hospital reminded me of few important things. I decided to make myself a list.

    Hospital reminders:

1. Shave your damn arms!
When I get the call for transplant I will bring the razor to the airport with me and shave in the car if I have to. I hate hospital tape.

2. Bring food for yourself.
Three days in the hospital and I lost three pounds. While this is a great dieting mechanism for some, I need calories! Calories calories! The hospital feeds me 3 times a day. That is not enough for me. I can't take the chance of losing weight. Bring butter and whole milk. I am not kidding. Because I am a cardiac patient, they send me low fat stuff, like fat free milk and margarine. Crap, I tell you. Waste of space in my stomach that is. They have no place in my diet. I need fat. Ask anyone who has seen me scarf down a fettuccine alfredo before 9:00 a.m. I may have heart problems, but cholesterol is not one of them.

3. Watch the doctors and the staff like a hawk.
Not because they don't know how to do their job, but because they can make mistakes. They do make mistakes. My life is held precariously in the balance. I need to watch what happens all the time. It's like a game of Pickup Sticks where you balance each stick on top the next, in hopes of not knocking the whole thing down. That's how I feel about the state of my health right now. I understand that one false move can make it all come tumbling down. I am watching. I am deliberate. I ask questions and make demands. I am the quintessential pain in the ass patient. I understand that the grim irony in that the same modern marvels of medicine that have managed to keep me alive will be the same thing that can do me in in the end. Can you blame me for being vigilant?

4. Take all the pain medication offered and then ask for more.
Pain is not my forte. I can't do pain. I can do suffering, sorrow, and loss. I can take it as long as it doesn't hurt. Then I am a wimp. I can suffer like nobody's business

for the long haul, but I shut down when things physically hurt. I thank God for anesthesiologists. My heart has been broken time and time again. I've learned that I can take the emotional pain. I keep reminding myself of what my brother and sister both said to me about my new heart never being broken like my old one. And that when the old heart is gone, all the heartbreak will go to. I hope like hell that they are right.

-- Liz

November, 2002

⟿

Friday, November 1, 2002

Today a very important date, worthy of note: Today I am finally eligible for Medicare!!! Sure it sounds like no big deal. But it really is. In order to become a beneficiary of this entitlement, I needed to survive long enough. Cost cutting at its American best.

Two years and 5 months to qualify from the date of disability. What a truly rotten system. If you can survive your "complete and permanent" disability long enough, you can become a recipient, too.

Now I may be responsible for $500- $800 per month for the immunosuppressants alone. This is still an insane amount of money, but much better than yesterday when the number was $800-$1200 per month. What's worse, yesterday they would not have covered the immunosuppressants at all if I had the surgery because it would have been before their official coverage date.

Ready for the biggest irony of all?

I almost can't even talk about any of this in fear of somehow jinxing myself... but here it goes: In the long run, it's actually cheaper to transplant me than to keep me going on the regimen I am currently on. (Can you see why on most days I want to pull my hair out?)

Now a couple more hurdles in the distance.... but for today, good news.

Phew, giant sign of relief.

-- Liz

<u>*Tuesday, November 5, 2002*</u>

This past Sunday there was a "Walk for Liz". Girlfriends from high school, family, and lovely strangers joined for a walk-a-thon at Jones Beach in Long Island. It was a wonderfully successful fundraiser held by my girlie pals from St Agnes High School.

Yes, I went an all-girl Catholic school in Queens, which of course would explain some of our more reckless behavior in life…. but I won't digress.(That would have to be its own website!)

They walked, and talked to me by phone, and I giggled and laughed while they got cold, tired, sore, hungry, and crabby…well, maybe not so much.

I wasn't able to walk with them…or even join them for that matter, but they promised to do it all over again when I could walk it on my own. I am looking forward to the day.

-- Liz

<u>*Thursday, November 7, 2002*</u>

"The only thing that makes life possible is permanent, intolerable uncertainty; not knowing what comes next."
-- URSULA K. LEGUIN

I imagine that one day this journal will end. Perhaps I will be transplanted, or miraculously cured. Maybe neither of these will happen.

I don't know how the story ends. I wish I did; I don't.

My impatient nature and my natural inability to delay gratification make this exercise in waiting harder than anything I could have ever imagined.

When I read a book, I quite often read the last page when I am in the vicinity of the end. It's just who I am. I then read the book through to the end. It's just what I do. I can't bear not knowing. I get so anxious I have to satisfy my need to know--now-- and then, I can peacefully return to the last chapter.

This is one time where I can't skip to the end and see what happens.

I can't help but wonder…as I struggle to understand my fate. I can't help but think that there is some greater life lesson here for me--in the waiting, I mean.

*I don't get it, as though it were some kind of inside joke. I wonder... **what is it that I don't get?***

Why AM I waiting so long?

There is part of me that thinks perhaps the perfect match will be out there for me when the time is right, and that is the reason for waiting. Maybe I needed to get well enough and strong enough to be prepared for my angel donor, so everything will be just perfect.

Then, there is part of me that thinks that perhaps I am waiting for some future scientific discovery that will magically make all my ills go "poof!"

The tragic part of me that thinks "Why me?" believes that I am just supposed to be doing what I doing, so that I can have peace and the time to say goodbye to the people I love.

Maybe I have not bargained sufficiently-- "If I get this transplant then I promise to climb the highest mountain, sail the stormy seas, find cures for cruel diseases like this one"-- but I don't have those grand aspirations. I don't think that's bad, though. Maybe my wish is too simple.

As my friend once said to me, "Is your heart beating today?" (Yes.)

"Is it going to stop beating today?" (I don't think so.)

"Well then", she proclaimed, "today is a great day!"

So if you see me walking around talking to myself like an old crazy lady, know that it's the serenity prayer I am muttering to myself, over and over.

-- Liz

<u>*Tuesday, November 12, 2002*</u>

I am going up on the soapbox.

A friend of mine once said to me "I swear Liz, the angrier I see you get, the better you become".

She is right.

Somewhere along the line I was told and made to believe that in order to heal I needed to be happy and positive all the time. I beg to differ. There is amazing energy in anger (and every other repressed emotion for that matter). And sometimes it doesn't matter where you get the energy. Energy heals. Not that you want to be angry all the time....but the ugly feelings need to be expressed, too, and then burn themselves out.

Somewhere along the way society and our culture has discovered (or rediscovered) the power we have in healing ourselves, which is a great thing. This societal mind shift went from how to make yourself healthy- to how are you making yourself ill? (Take your pick--stress, anger, diet, what you avoid, what you indulge in.) But this is also a great thing, as it can lead us to the "on /off" switch of what brought us to our illness. I have learned we have an outrageous amount of power over our well-being.

But unfortunately this can also be a dangerous and loaded concept as far as I am concerned. Laying all this responsibility on people to stay positive upbeat and heal themselves can end up making people feel inadequate and guilty;--as though they are doing something wrong, and in turn keeping themselves from being well. It's not so simple, nor so black and white; and the answer, I am sure, lies somewhere in between.

I am not going to deny that stress and misery can be hurtful--because I know first-hand that it can be. What I am saying is that we have to be careful not blame ourselves for not healing ourselves. Realize that ugly feelings like sadness--and yes, anger--have a place in healing. Just because they are negative feelings doesn't mean they can't become a positive force.

Anger has worked wonders for me. I won't deny it. I **can't** deny it. It is not the undercurrent or mainstay of my life. But is has been a tremendous vehicle. I have allowed myself to be angry - given myself permission. It is rare to give ourselves permission to be "ugly" because generally we think of anger as something that sucks energy out of you—"a waste of time and energy", as the saying goes. Sometimes it is, but I don't think it always is.

I think of it as a fire that needs to burn itself out. Give it oxygen. Let it burn. Then **poof!** --it will be gone.

-- Liz

Thursday, November 14, 2002

We got the girls a kitten. We finally caved in. Emma had been asking for one since her birthday. Initially we told her that we'd get her one "after the transplant". She hounded us and harassed us. She cut pictures out of kittens; we bought her stuffed *animals. She looked them up for hours at a time on the computer; we'd print them out for her to cut out and paste in her bedroom. Finally she cut a deal with us: a kitten by her half-birthday (Oct. 7), regardless of a transplant. She told everyone--friends, family, neighbors, and teachers that on Oct.7, she would be getting a kitten. It seemed so far away at the time. I thought for sure that I would have been transplanted by now. No such luck. Oct. 7 came and went and by the 27th, little Mr. Kitty, aka "Pooh", came to live with us.*

So what am I crazy? Probably. Guilt ridden? Yep, a little of that, too.

So now, I have this itty-bitty fur ball following me around the house, nibbling at my cords, getting his neck wrapped up in them, and then running away from me. But oh, he is so cute!

Luci wants a dog. This won't be happening anytime soon. So being the resourceful child of mine that she is, she has managed to borrow a neighbor's dog for outings every few days. Luci claims she owns "half a dog". She walks the dog and therefore has given herself the title of "part-time dog owner". The dog and her owner both seem pretty happy with the arrangement so far, too. Today I volunteered at the girls' school library.

Life has been suspiciously "normal" as of late...but you won't find me questioning it.

-- Liz

<u>*Friday, November 15, 2002*</u>

> *"Life shrinks or expands in proportion to one's courage."*
> *-- ANAIS NIN*

<u>*Saturday, November 16, 2002*</u>
"The Phone Finally Rings!"

It was an icy windy night when the surgeon called me. I was in New York City for a Doctor appointment (Ironic, eh?)

There was also an educational forum at Mt. Sinai given by the Scleroderma Foundation. Because the weather did not look good, I decided to join some friends from the local scleroderma support group, who were also going to the forum, and then take the bus home.

I went to the forum (which was wonderful) then went to my mother's for dinner; we watched some TV and went to bed. I said goodnight to Scott and the children by phone and hung up. Then I called him back and said, "Don't forget to answer the phone if it rings tonight."

"You know I don't hear the phone in my sleep", he joked with me.

I myself was asleep by 10 p.m.

I received the phone call from the surgeon at about 11:30 p.m., and then it gets foggy from there.

Basically if it had been a Hollywood movie it would have gone like this:

Girl gets call and offer of a donor.

Girl calls pilot, confirms that there is someone to fly her to her life saving surgery.

Doctor calls back and says that pilot has determined that it is too windy, too icy to fly. He tells the girl that there will be no surgery, and that there will be a next time. "Unfortunate circumstances", he consoles her. Girl cries, hangs up the phone.

Girl calls around. In a few minute she has found another pilot with a bigger airplane (a jet) who tells her he CAN fly her.

Girl calls back the Doctor and triumphantly tells him that she now has a plane ... (the audience cheers)

She flies off into the sunset ...

But remember this is MY life we are talking about ...

So the movie follows the same time line of events, except when girl calls the doctor back to tell him that she has found a another pilot. Yes I called and found a jet to charter to Pittsburgh at midnight on a Saturday night (only in New York City), she finds out the organs have been offered to someone else.

But all hope is not gone yet, she is told, because the candidate has not accepted or rejected the offer yet. If they decline, they can re-offer the organs to girl.

Girl and family wait approximately an hour like this, with everything hanging in the balance, until finally they are told definitively and without a doubt, that the other person has accepted the offer.

Girl sobs in her mother's arms.

Not a movie I'd pay to see that's for sure.

So, I went to sleep (eventually), listening to the wind howl, the rain and hail pelting the ground. When I woke, the sky was quiet and clear. It all seemed

very unreal and dreamlike except for the terrible awful feeling in the pit of my stomach.
    -- Liz

Tuesday, November 19, 2002
I am home dealing with my devastating disappointment... I am emotionally fraught and worn thin, but trying my best to make sense out of something I can't make sense out of.
    -- Liz

Wednesday, November 20, 2002
And yes. I even shaved my arms...
    -- Liz

Friday, November 22, 2002
> *"There are very few human beings who receive the truth, complete and staggering, by instant illumination. Most of them acquire it fragment by fragment, on a small scale, by successive developments, cellularly, like a laborious mosaic"*
> *-- ANAIS NIN*

Sunday, November 24, 2002
Yesterday was my goddaughter's 1st birthday. I missed her party. I was supposed be in New York for it. But I just couldn't make it.

The anxiety has been constant. The tap, tap, tapping in the back of my head has become louder and more insistent since last Saturday's call.

I couldn't do it, even though Scott assures me that there was no way I could have left from Binghamton even if I had been home; that really my best chance was from New York City.

But I couldn't do it.

I don't know how I will make through the winter- I remind myself that its only November. Many more dark, cold and snowy nights to come.

Much angst.

I am not sure I can shake this off yet.

So what? What am I going to do? Be a prisoner of my own home? Too paranoid to venture out? Not a chance. Instead I went out last night and spent some time with friends. Thank goodness for the normalcy of relationships. I don't know what I would do without my friends.

On a positive note, I have since last week managed to do most of my Christmas shopping. That's what fear does to me, it makes me shop. (Ha!)

I did it last year, too, at the same pace. As if somehow, someway, that makes me in more control of anything… it doesn't. But having everything done by Thanksgiving does make the holiday more pleasant to enjoy with friends and family.

So I am busy wrapping now.

-- Liz

<u>*Thursday, November 28, 2002*</u>

I am thankful for the ability to walk, even though I can't make it too far.

I am thankful for the ability to breathe better.

I am thankful for the chance to sit up in chair, rather than having to lay down all the time.

I am thankful for the energy to get to and from my car, so that I can drive my family and me places that we wish to go.

I am thankful for the opportunity to bend over and pick up things if I need to (although I don't really like to; I get dizzy and out of breath). But at least I can physically do it.

I am thankful for the chance to eat to my heart's content.

I am thankful for my family, because they love me even though I am so crabby (Department of Understatement) and I love them more than they'll ever know.

I am even thankful for the "call" I received, because it means that my chance is coming. Someone else needed those organs more than me this time around (two people actually, is what I was told--the heart went to one person and the lungs to another.)

But most of all, I am thankful to the people I love and that love me, because they help keep the fire burning inside me, and without them cheering me on, it would have blown out long ago.

Now really, what's better than a holiday that gives us the chance to overeat with people we love?

Happy Thanksgiving

-- Liz

December, 2002

$\backsim$

> *"The stories are here, they are all in here, there are no*
> *locks on the storybox, on storybox, on storybox…"*
> *-- THE MAGIC GARDEN (FOR ALL WHO ARE PRODUCTS*
> *OF NEW YORK CITY IN THE 70'S)*

When I graduated from college, my then-boyfriend (now husband), my girl-friend, and I decided we were going to leave New York and live somewhere else.

We each picked a different city, and then did out homework. Our job was to research and then "sell" our city to the other two. The three cities that we picked were Seattle, Washington, Flagstaff, Arizona, and Santa Fe, New Mexico.

We couldn't decide. So we ended up putting the ol' blindfold on and putting our finger down on the map. That's how we chose to live in Santa Fe. We decided on a date and then we packed everything we owned into his very small Honda Accord hatchback and headed out west.

On the way there we stopped to visit friends of ours who lived in Jackson Hole, Wyoming.

They were excited to have us visit, and decided that we should go hiking in Grand Teton National Park for a few days.

Our gracious hosts then surprised us when we arrived by telling us that our hike would include llamas. Yes, llamas. Marco and Darwin were their names (I won't soon forget).

Marco and Darwin's job was to carry our food and supplies for the next 4 days while we hiked through the park.

This sounded like a great idea. We learned "Llama 101" basics--how to take care of them, how to pack them and how to understand their behavior. We also learned quickly that when they are unhappy, they 1. Don't cooperate, and 2. Spit at you when they are really ticked. So we learned, really fast, as you might imagine, how to duck and run for cover.

It was a difficult trip--more accurately known as "Our Trip from Hell".

It was also very beautiful.

It was the middle of October, cold and raining, and at the highest altitudes, snowing. I had terrible altitude sickness and was having trouble eating and drinking.

But we had to keep a certain pace. We had to cover a certain number of miles each day in order to get out of the park on time (our last day in the park was the last day for the season), so we had to keep moving. It got harder and harder on all of us.

The llamas were also having a hard time keeping up. When they were too tired, they would refuse to walk. They would literally dig in their heels.

At first we were kind and cajoled them. When they were crabby, they would prepare to hurl a "loogie" at us, and we would run out of their spitting distance screaming, and hide behind each other. Climbing up, up, up was exhausting, I just kept thinking, **don't worry Liz there will be down, down, down and then everything will be ok.**

But it just didn't happen that way. And of course as you might imagine, it got even harder. By the fourth day, I knew that we would be finishing and therefore felt relief. Of course, it turned out to be the hardest day of all. We ended up climbing more. I was in disbelief. How come, if this trip was coming to an end, were we still going up, instead of down? It was defying my logic. (By now you get where I am going right?)

Finally, we decided that since the park was closing at sunset it was in our best interest to split up; My boyfriend and I would take the llamas and go at our own pace and our friends would get out of the park, get the truck and meet us at the trailhead.

That left us with two very cranky llamas. I thought we were finally coming out of the woods when we found ourselves on a switch back in place called Devils Canyon. A very accurately named pass that resembled –yes--Hell.

We were probably 14,000 feet up on this switch back, and as I said I was terribly nauseous and dizzy and on this itty-bitty gravel switch back about 12 inches wide, with a very serious phobia of heights. The wind was so intense that I thought for sure it would blow me off the mountain.

I decided that the best way was to crawl. It was either that, throw up, or be blown off the side of the mountain. So there I was, on my hands and knees, crawling up this switch back with the cranky llama in tow.

I was not a happy camper.

I muttered, cursed and cried. I cursed the llamas for being so uncooperative and asked God to strike down our gracious friends. Eventually, I just started conversing with God and asking questions, and pretty quickly this evolved into hollering. "Why are you doing this to me God? What did I do to deserve this?' and other stupid questions for which there are no answers. Indignantly, I added "Don't you know that I'm just a girl from Queens?"

All of which of course was not exactly stellar "date behavior" on my part. But I realized on that trip that I didn't need the great outdoors to have an adventure. All I needed were friends, and a restaurant that serves drinks with pretty umbrellas in them.

And the point to this story? Oh, yeah…the point. The point is that I wish I could scream it all over again from the highest mountain. Although the feelings would be different, I have a sneaking suspicion the dialogue would be the same.

*So instead I will just think it…REALLY LOUDLY…**Please God I beg you… I am just a girl from Queens…***

And oh yes…. when we finally made it down, we reconvened and debriefed from this very traumatic event at the very appropriately named Lame Duck Chinese Restaurant.

With pretty umbrella drinks, of course.

-- Liz

<u>Sunday, December 8, 2002</u>

> *"Woke up, fell out of bed,*
> *Dragged a comb across my head*
> *Found my way downstairs and drank a cup,*
> *And looking up I noticed I was late.*
> *Found my coat and grabbed my hat*
> *Made the bus in seconds flat*
> *Found my way upstairs and had a smoke,*
> *Somebody spoke and I went into a dream."*
> *-- A DAY IN THE LIFE (LENNON/MCCARTNEY)*

I cut my line Friday morning by accident. My central line, my Hickman Catheter! It is the line that delivers the medicine to my heart. I took a shower and was changing my dressing; the tape was stuck, so I took a scissor to it.

One small snip! -- And the damage was done. As I watched the blood start pouring out of my chest, I assessed the situation. "My immediate thoughts were Oh my God. Tape it. Get dressed. Call Scott. Go to hospital. And then within seconds, blood was shooting out all over the place. I had to reassess the situation. I shortened my "to do" list:

Get dressed.

Call 911.

The girls, who can't stand the sight of blood, were crying and sobbing. I told them I was going to the hospital, the ambulance was coming, that I wasn't sick- I had cut my cord. I told them to get dressed for school, which they did (in record time). Brushing their hair and crying at the same time, they promptly fled to my neighbor's house. (Oh the damage done, my poor little babies.... it breaks my heart).

The ambulance arrived in minutes; they restarted my lines in my arm pretty quickly (thankfully), and then took me to the hospital. I cried all the way there, as I knew that the line could not be saved or fixed. I would need to have it replaced (AGAIN)--and it was of my own doing.

The nurses clamped the end down, and taped the clamp to my chest until I was able to have the surgery the next day.

Since then, I have caught some serious abuse about my ability to handle sharp objects from my family, friends and even the nurses and doctors in the hospital.

In one quick "snip", I ruined what was supposed to be a very busy but nice weekend filled with holiday cheer. We were supposed to celebrate my husband's birthday with friends.

It's the collateral damage that I wreak upon my own family that I can't cope with. Worse, I did it to myself.

So while my body is busy being sore and healing, my ego will, without a doubt, take a little longer.

-- Liz

Wednesday, December 11, 2002

Last week's whole scene was reminiscent of an incident I had a year ago were I stabbed myself in the hand. Same set up.

That time, I was frustrated with a plastic juice bottle. My girls had come home from school and wanted a snack. I couldn't get the lid off. In my frustration I took a knife to it. Put it right through my hand. Blood everywhere. It sent the girls running to the neighbor's house. Blood, ambulance, hospital--same set up.

Now am I really that accident-prone? I don't think so. I think it's a combination of frustration and being physically weak that combine to make me do to super stupid things.

Now I have been banned by the powers that be, namely my father-in-law (who comes every time to the hospital and shows me which gray hair I am now responsible for) from all sharp objects. I received a pair of safety scissors as a gift instead.

-- Liz

Monday, December 16, 2002

My girlfriend came over Friday morning and helped me wrap gifts. We had tea; I mixed my medicine while she wrapped the gifts. Yes--wrapping gifts leaves me out of breath. Then I went to the Doctor to have my stitches removed, and have some blood work taken that needed to be sent to Pittsburgh. They didn't have the correct tubes; they had to courier them to the office from the hospital. I went to a cookie *exchange, and had some yummy soup with other moms from the girls' school. Then, I left the party, and went back to the doctor's office to have the blood drawn. They still did not have the tube. I waited some more.*

When I got home I dove into bed for a quick nap before the girls returned home from school. Later, I went out to dinner with Scott. All in all, a very busy day for me...too much.

It's like this: most people get a tank full of energy every day to use. (Like gasoline) Nowadays I get about one-quarter-tank. That's not bad. I used to get less. On many days I don't get any "gas" at all. But I just have to remember to use it judiciously-- a lesson I constantly learn and then have to relearn.

Oh how I long for a normal "to do" list...

-- Liz

<u>*Wednesday, December 18, 2002*</u>

*Pondering my "to do" list I can't help but think, **why can't I be happy with the little I have? Can't that be enough?** Sometimes I think that maybe I am selfish for wanting more out of life. Really- I could be content with what I have, **if** I could have the guarantee of breath. I don't have that guarantee. But I wouldn't necessarily have that with a transplant either. But my rational brain tells me I could be screwed either way. In my heart, I know the answer. I am choosing a transplant because I am willing to take that risk in order to have the privilege of more time with my girls. I want to see time pass, watch them grow up, and most importantly, be there for them. A Transplant gives me the hope that I will be there for them.*

This has been an immensely difficult year on our family emotionally, with many external factors that were out of my control. I acknowledge that there always will be plenty more factors out of my control in the future--but I vowed to myself then (and now) that I would never allow myself to be taken to this dark abyss again. If I go again it will be because I am choosing to take myself there.

Yes, please; I'd like one ticket to the dark abyss of my psyche?'...*not likely to happen. You won't find a hyperlink titled "The Dark Abyss of Your Psyche" on Travelocity.com anytime soon either.*

Regardless, my point is-- I am not clicking on it.

I am choosing to enjoy my holidays, family, and friends (in spite of the fact that I am danger to myself).

And I will spend some time New York City, too. After talking with the transplant coordinator at some length, she convinced me that there's nothing to fear should I get called again while there.

"Think about it", she said. "Now you know exactly what to do."

-- Liz

Friday, December 20, 2002

> *"I believe that we are solely responsible for our choices, and we have to accept the consequences of every deed, word, and thought throughout our lifetime."*
>
> *-- ELIZABETH KÜBLER-ROSS*

Friday, December 20, 2002

This just in from the Department of Doom and Gloom: I have an infection in my new Hickman catheter.

I spent the day at the doctor's and the hospital. They have taken the tests and cultures necessary to determine what exactly is growing. Best-case scenario: a couple of weeks' worth of antibiotics. Worst-case scenario: change the line, again. Oh my God. Can I really go through that again?

In-between scenarios include a blast of some very expensive antibiotic (that the pharmacy has now ordered for me in case I need it), and insertion of a PICC line to deliver IV antibiotics for 3 weeks. The nurse has me scheduled at outpatient surgery for 11:00 a.m. Monday Christmas eve, in case I need it.

Now I have to wait until Monday morning to see exactly what is planned for me.

I am tired. I am so tired. I am so very tired...

I am saying my prayers and asking for yours. Please please please. I need a break.

-- Liz

<u>*Saturday, December 21, 2002*</u>

This just in:

I talked with the transplant coordinator, if I need a PICC line, then I will be taken off the transplant list for the three weeks of treatment. Now I don't mean to be morbid, but this is the busy season for transplant centers. If I need something more than oral antibiotics, I will be "inactivated".

There's nothing I can type that expresses my feelings right now.

-- Liz

<u>*Sunday, December 22, 2002*</u>

The Doctor called today.

I only need the two weeks' worth of oral antibiotics!!!!!!!!!!!!!

Phew! Phew! Phew!

I am off the hook.

Thank you so much (once again) for all the support and prayers.

Merry Christmas to all!

-- Liz

January, 2003

◦

<u>Friday, January 3, 2003</u>

We made it home today from the holidays with our families. It was a well-deserved, wonderful holiday. The snow is coming down hard and fast now, but we are snug and cozy in our home.

We left New York last night, and made it about halfway home before abandoning our trip--it was too icy. So we stopped at a hotel, (the girls loved that!)And finished the trip this morning- phew!

My antibiotics seem to be working just fine. All is good and bright. This trip home was bittersweet. My mother is moving from the house we all grew up in. So it was our last trip "home". We celebrated over 30 years' worth of Christmases at that house...so, as I said, it was bittersweet.

Now I am settling in to watch the pretty snowfall--a few days' worth and a few feet from what I hear--and the nicest part of all is that is not even ruffling my feathers; that's always a nice change.

Happy New Year!

-- Liz

<u>Saturday, January 4, 2003</u>
A lovely quote to start the New Year:

-- Liz

"God turns you from one feeling to another and teaches by means of opposites, so that you have two wings to fly, not one."
-- RUMI QUOTED IN LOVE IS A FIRE BY LLEWELLYN VAUGHAN-LEE

<u>*Wednesday, January 8, 2003*</u>
Why do people want to read this journal? It's a question I often ask myself. Moreover, why would I choose to share my sorry life story in such a public way?

I read it sometimes and all I can think is…finger down the back of my throat, pathetic! YIKES. Run away!

When the transplant team first mentioned fundraising to us, I never thought for a moment, "Hey! I think that I'll fundraise by sharing my private most intimate thoughts on the World Wide Web!" It was never intended that way.

Its intent was initially to fundraise, and to share information about my journey. And miraculously, while it's done both of those things, it has also somehow engaged me into a very public/ private, and at times surreal, exercise in self-awareness and gratitude. Somewhere out of that it grew into something much more meaningful--for me, and for the people that read it (or at least so I am told). It has grown to be a blessing.

So aside from wanting to know what's going one with me, why DO people read this?

Here are the best reasons I can conjure up:

1. *We all have our own sadness and joys. Reading (and writing) this journal is a way to validate those feelings- both good and bad. I think we are all given the same "boxes" in life- they just come wrapped in different paper. So my losses are someone else's loss, as are my triumphs, joys and hope. Ye old collective experience. Same box, different presentation. I know this brings ME comfort.*

2. *People read it and it provides perspective. They realize, "Jeez, I don't have it that bad!" or, "I have nothing to complain about." Or as my friend Joe says, "Liz, you have cornered the market for disease and bad luck, no one can be as sick as you, or complain about ANYTHING in your presence either." (He then triumphantly crowned me the Queen of Autoimmune Diseases). And it's true--people often say, "I feel so badly complaining to you; like you don't have enough on your plate." I tell them no way. It's nice*

to hear other people's complaints. I welcome tales of woe that are not my own. In reading my story, there is the realization that, for better or worse, anyone can get sick just like I did. Pretty much overnight, with little warning. No one wants to think about that though. Contrary to what "healthy" (and I use the term loosely) people want to think, the world is not made up of two teams--the sick and the well.

Sometimes the well get sick and the sick get well. I got a bum deal and a ticket to the Land of The Unwell. I am hoping it's a round trip ticket. But I know the reality can be a one-way ticket. I think reading this journal reminds people that they too may have to make a trip to the Land of The Unwell--either for themselves or for someone they love. My hope is, of course, that everyone is fortunate enough to get a round-trip ticket.

Besides, take it from me, it's a crappy place to visit and you wouldn't want to live there.

-- Liz

Wednesday, January 15, 2003

My Canadian transplant soul sister Allison has received notice that she has now moved to the number 2 spot for a double lung transplant.

This is REALLY exciting news.

-- Liz

Tuesday, January 21, 2003

The Itch is back. I itch and I scratch and I itch. ALL OVER. In the past, it was completely intolerable. It's not nearly as bad now, but I have been spending hours in bed entertaining 'The Itch'. I am not sure what causes it; my guess is some type of side effect from all the medicines. When I met the woman with pulmonary hyper-tension (with identical medicines- IV and all) that had just had her transplant, that was the first question I asked her. Not- "How are you breathing?" Or, "How are you feeling?" But do you itch?

"Not anymore", she happily reported as she showed me the scars and scabs on her legs. It stopped as soon as she received her transplant.

The itch keeps me awake. Last year I remember being in the hospital bed, and the itch tormenting me to the point where scratched myself raw and bloody. But I couldn't care less; so the staff gave me some serious sedatives to make me leave myself alone.

I hate the itch.

AND I hate this cold. It freezes my damn cords. But at least that gives something other than the itch to think about.

-- Liz

<u>Monday, January 27, 2003</u>

Being sick is time consuming.

Both the girls and I have been thru a stomach virus, that's has kept us all very busy.

Just as we thought it was over, we got to go around the carousel again.

I am very used to my own limitations at this point, but to add my sick girls to the mix made it very obvious to me how hard it is too keep up.

I think we are back to "normal", whatever that is.

-- Liz

<u>Tuesday, January 28, 2003</u>

Candy of the Week:

Jolly Rancher Gummies (!!)

-- Liz

<u>Friday, January 31, 2003</u>

I have been busy sleeping. Soundly. Napping for long periods of time.

I don't know what it is, as only the month of January can do to a person. It's like someone has sprinkled fairy dust on me, I can't stay awake.

Every time I lie down, I pass out. It's not a bad thing, it's like nesting or cocooning, I am not sure which.

A psychic once told me that I would write something, something that would be many pages.

"Very large", she said.

I laughed. I wouldn't write anything that I didn't have to- I couldn't imagine committing myself to any sort of large writing project.

All of a sudden she was right. Shows you what I know.

-- Liz

February, 2003

_6_

<u>Wednesday, February 5, 2003</u>

W hen children see my bag they ask questions. Lots of them. When adults look at my medical apparatus, most avert their eyes. But kids get right to the heart of the matter- no pun intended.

What's that?

-That my medicine…

What's it for?

-To help my lungs and heart….

Does your heart not beat?

-No my heart beats- just not as well as everyone else's.

"Oh", they answer, and that's the end of that. Usually that is as much information as they need- they are satisfied- they walk away.

Emma once described my cords to her friend in a manner I had never considered.

She explained smiling: "My mom is lucky she doesn't have to take yucky-tasting medicine--she gets it right through her cords so she doesn't have to take pills or swallow anything." There's nothing clearer in this world than kid's perspective.

Now adults are a different story. Perhaps they do it out of discomfort, or maybe even respect. I wish, however, that they would ask instead of averting their eyes. It takes so much more energy to ignore, or pretend to ignore, my very obvious medical contraption. It's like ignoring the pink elephant in the living room.

-- Liz

Friday, February 7, 2003
My daughter Emma has been home sick with a fever for the last 4 days...she says,
"Mom don't talk to me- I am too tired to talk."

That would be one very sick child who doesn't want to chat, chat, chat the day
away.

So I am exhausted, and I miss writing in this journal...hopefully I can come
back soon...that is if no one else catches "it" next.
-- Liz

Monday, February 10, 2003
Another day, another daughter.

Now my Luci is sick. She has pinkeye and multitude of other symptoms, but
no fever-yet.

Miraculously I am doing ok. No fever, no congestion. It's a little strange.
Usually if I even drive past a rogue germ, I catch it. But so far, so good.

Take no small thing for granted, that's what I say.
-- Liz

Tuesday, February 11, 2003
Luci has a fever today.... but I am still hanging in there.

Next week, Scott and I are going to Pittsburgh for a doctor's appointment, a
routine checkup. I was speaking with my transplant coordinator about our upcom-
ing visit. She told me that they almost had an offer for me this past weekend. She
almost called me, but then found out the organs were not as good as they needed to
be. Fortunately, she said, she never even got to call me. This is just as well, because
its sounds like it would have been another false alarm.

Hum, how did this make feel? I asked myself when I hung up. I decided that
it made feel happy and hopeful.
-- Liz

Sunday, February 16, 2003
I watched a video of my baby shower yesterday with my girls. I see myself 10 years
ago, laughing happily with my friends and family. I am glowing with the excite-
ment that only a new mother has.

It seems so long ago; I think to myself, a world and a lifetime ago. I am reminded of the childhood I had pictured and dreamed of for my child and then later – children…I acknowledge to myself that it didn't exactly turn out as I had envisioned.

Inevitably, the sadness and disappointment that comes with that acknowledgment sinks in. I didn't really plan on something like a rare progressive and incurable disease. But the reality is, is that it changes that family picture dramatically.

I acknowledge to myself that there are plenty of reasons out there that also change this picture for families; things like a sudden death, divorce, separation, or even violence within a family can change the dreams and hopes we had for our loved ones drastically and suddenly. I am certain that I am not alone with this feeling. For many families, it's just becomes part of normal family development.

And anybody who's ever had this type of experience knows that there is a certain amount of loss involved when you have to say goodbye to that "family portrait" which was in your mind.

Sometimes we make deliberate choices that change the outcome of our family structure. Sometimes the changes are completely out of our hands, as in the case of my illness.

But what I had envisioned for my children, no matter how small and inconsequential, or large and significant, didn't exactly pan out the way I thought it would. And that's a loss I have to grieve.

And when on a bad day I sit around blaming myself for the life I wish they had, I remind myself, that my children have other things that are just as, or even more, important and valuable.

My secret wish is that they don't grow up to view it in the same way. I don't want them to grow up resenting "the mother they never had". I want them to remember the loving mother they did have.

My hopes are that they remember the good, the love, the fun, and all the positive things that came from this uncharted change in plans.

(Of course, I realize it may take years of therapy!!!!)

I guess my point is I do the best I can with what I can. We all do. I just hope that is good enough for my children to have not only a happy healthy childhood, but a meaningful adulthood as well.

I am not looking to candy-coat their life either. I want them to remember the hard and the ugly parts, along with "warm fuzzy" feelings. Life is not a

perpetual "Kodak Moment", regardless of what the media and our culture relent-
lessly drums into our skulls. And I want them to know that it's OK to be sad, or
mad, or whatever. I truly believe those unpleasant times in our lives help us become
who we are meant to be.

My hope is simple for my girls: That they grow up to be well-adjusted, happy
adults who recognize and appreciate all that is "so good" in life as good, and that
all that is "so bad" in life as not necessarily...bad.

Sometimes messy can be good.

-- Liz

Monday, February 17, 2003

The headline of today's paper reads, "Massive Snowstorm Pummels Eastern US".

We are supposed to fly out to Pittsburgh tomorrow--HA ha ha ha ha ... (that's
an insane laugh, not a "tee-hee-hee" - kind of laugh.)

Figures.

...Ha ha ha ha...... ha.

-- Liz

Wednesday, February 19, 2003

We postponed our trip to Pittsburgh. We will try again in a few weeks.

Perhaps next time there won't be a blizzard in our way.

Right about now I am asking myself, Damn, Liz why won't you move to Pittsburgh
and cut yourself some slack? I mean it's only your life we are talking about here.

Believe me; I go back and forth on this all the time. The staff and doctors have
thus far encouraged me to stay home for 2 important reasons:

1- Because the scarcity of the surgery. They have only done two heart/lung
transplants this year and the chances of it being my blood type (B) are REALLY
slim. Last year they did over one thousand Lung Transplants in the United
States. They did thirty three, yes you read that right, heart/ lung transplants.
Of the thirty three transplanted, **5**, were blood type B. The bottom line is I never
really know when they will call--which is different from lungs alone, where
generally they'll call you to move if they think you have a wait time of 6 months
or less.

2- They understand how important my family is to me--how much I depend on them and how much they depend on me.

I have to deal with disappointment. Again.

-- Liz

<u>Wednesday, February 26, 2003</u>

Poor, poor Jesica (yes, with one's'). What an organ donation story of tragedy for her and her family. How could they transplant her with organs not of her blood type? So many hopes, for so many years. They trusted the doctors as any one of us would. She waited 3 years for the first set organs and a few days for the next set. Unfortunately, her body was not able to handle all of that trauma.

I think that speaks to 2 higher powers-- The first and foremost of which is the power of God.

The second is the amazing role media can play in organ donation. If it hadn't been such a huge news story, all the "would-be" l donors would not have known of her plight. The family that donated the organs did not specify that they were for Jesica. However, there is no doubt in my mind that her second donor was a direct result of the "far-reaching" power of the media. In the end, I hope all the media attention does not do the opposite--put people off and discourage them from donating.

Only one-third of potential donors (people who are brain dead and therefore possible candidates) actually donate their organs when it comes right down to it. Of that 30%, only 15-18% of those lungs are actually viable for transplant. Those are crazy statistics that demonstrate not only the scarcity of organs in our country, but the privilege it is for anyone to even get a transplant.

Unfortunately, Jesica's transplant was a miracle; but one with a tragic ending.

The whole thing reminds me of what my daughter Luci, then 7-years-old, said to me 2 years ago:

"Mom doctors don't know everything do they?"

Regretfully I had to answer honestly. "No they don't".

In the meantime, my family has suggested that I invest in a good permanent marker to write my blood type "B" across my chest when my time comes.

And I just might…

-- Liz

March 2003

_____

*M*y bizarro life provided me with a magical little twist this weekend. I was able to participate in a dance performance without being able to dance. (Huh?)

An organization called The Little Dance Company That Could in Binghamton, NY danced to one of my journal entries. It was a fundraiser for the local Crime Victims Assistance Center. Women's issues were a part of the performance. The piece was danced to a recording of me reading my entry of February 16. It was, as I said, bizarre, yet fascinating to somehow manage to take part in a dance performance. It was also very touching, and left me in tears. My friend asked my permission to cry during it (no one ever wants to cry in front of me). She sat next to me and whimpered her way through it. Really, it was quite lovely.

Just more proof that Angels are everywhere, and most importantly, where you least expect. My job is simply to be grateful-- and that I am.

In the meantime, we will try to go to Pittsburgh again this week. I look forward, as always, to the possibility of hearing some good news.

-- Liz

Monday, March 10, 2003

My right ventricle keeps growing.

Before I went to Pittsburgh, I had requested some tests to see if the status of my heart had possibly changed (that's me--always in hope of a double lung, instead of heart/ lung.) The doctor said that he would consider it, but warned me to not be "too hopeful".

When I went in for my appointment, the doctor was amazed to see how well I looked. He was so pleased; he was beside himself, smiling. He agreed to let me have further testing.

The initial results are not great though. While the hope was that my right ventricle had diminished in size (or at least stayed the same), it has in fact grown more. So much so, that the technician with the infamous bedside manner said to me, "Theoretically Liz, you shouldn't be up and walking."

And that's crazy you see, because not only am I up and walking I am walking greater distances with greater stamina than ever.

Normally, the right ventricle is half the size of the left ventricle. In my case my right ventricle is twice the size of the left ventricle. And not only is it big, but it is taking over the space of the left ventricle compressing it, compromising its ability to function as well. Not good news.

I will find out more in a few days. I am trying to keep my fear at bay until then.
-- Liz

<u>Wednesday, March 12, 2003</u>

> "Let us not look back in anger or forward in
> fear, but around in awareness."
> -- JAMES THURBER

(I am trying, I am trying)
-- Liz

<u>Saturday, March 15, 2003</u>
The doctor believes that the changes in my heart size are not significant enough to warrant any changes in my current medical regimen. So, the somewhat good news is that I won't be falling over from a heart attack any time soon (or sooner, as it were). The somewhat bad news is that I need to let my dream of having only a double lung transplant--go.

Other good news has to do with my Panel Reactive Antibody (PRA) level:

What is it? The percentage of cells from a panel of blood donors against which a potential recipient's serum reacts. The PRA reflects the percentage of the general population that a potential recipient makes antibodies (is sensitized) against. The higher the PRA, the less chance there is of finding a compatible organ donor.

They thought it was high 29/32; I had it retested and it is now lower, 14/18, which is really good news.

When I was told initially I needed a heart/ lung transplant I thought it was no big deal. I mean, what's adding one more organ if they are already going in? I didn't understand the complexity that adding a heart to the mix makes, and as a result, how much more rare the surgery becomes. Patients undergoing "Lung-only" transplants have better survival rates both during the procedure and post-transplant; who wouldn't be striving for that?? Hence my ongoing wish for "just lungs".

At any rate, the relief of knowing that I am really ok (for now) is worth so much more to me. Right now. Today.

-- Liz

<u>Wednesday, March 19, 2003</u>

> "Learn to get in touch with the silence within yourself, and know that everything in life has purpose. There are no mistakes, no coincidences, all events are blessings given to us to learn from."
> -- ELIZABETH KÜBLER-ROSS

I think about that crazy day of my false alarm call for the "transplant that wasn't". I laugh in retrospect at some of the events that ensued that day.

When I went to the educational forum on scleroderma, one of the speakers there was a doctor and researcher from Pittsburgh (of all places).

When she was asked where she gets her information for her research, she answered that it was from the "old lungs" of patients that had transplants.

After her session, I went up to meet her. I introduced myself, my heart, and my lungs to her, and told her that hopefully soon she would be examining my lungs. We laughed and she said that after I am transplanted and mobile in the hospital, I should have her paged and she would show me my old organs under the microscope. I said "Wow, how cool is that?" What I should have been saying is "Hey, can you give me a ride to Pittsburgh?". Ah, but the hand of fate works in very mysterious and crazy ways.

When "the call" came, I immediately called my brother, and he was out in Eastern Long Island. He made the ride back to Woodside in the pouring rain and ice in about 20 minutes. No small feat, as anyone who knows the Long Island Expressway can attest.

When I was told I would need to wait until the other person accepted or declined the organs, our collective mood went up, down, all around. Nervousness and excitement filled us all. We joked about the new personality traits that might come with the new organs... perhaps I would have a new craving for pickled eggs. My brother thought that perhaps I would feel the need to line dance. We laughed and were reminded solemnly (by my brother of all people) of the family that was out there right now suffering through the loss of someone they loved. This sobered us up quick. We prayed for them.

Then finally, when we were told that the other family had accepted the donor, we got ourselves ready for bed. It was at that point that I realized that during the whole ordeal, my mother was busy doing her own thing. She had made the beds. Cleaned up the house, emptied the kitty litter and cleaned out the fridge, putting most of the food in the freezer. I said, "Mom you froze all our food?"

She shrugged her shoulders and said, "What--I am going to let good food go to waste while we are gone?" I shrugged my shoulders back.

We all do what we got to do when the proverbial shit hits the fan, I guess. I call pilots; my mother makes beds and freezes food.

More importantly, I now understand that the transplant I was offered was not meant for me. Just maybe someone needed it more than me, or perhaps there is a more perfect match for me out there. I have to believe this. (Otherwise, I may go nuts).

-- Liz

<u>Sunday, March 23, 2003</u>
Life is so precious to me. I comfortably watch the war on TV from my couch eating Chinese food. Initially, I watch "Shock and Awe" like it's some kind of impressive fireworks display.

But within seconds I am squirming sitting there, knowing so many people will die and so many more will suffer (here, there, everywhere). Unreal at one level, all too real at another level.

The irony is not lost on me. I struggle to live, as I watch others die. It seems insane to me. I am watching the world go about its business of killing one and another, while I wait for the most important, lifesaving phone call of my entire life.

So unreal.

*I can't help but wonder, **why I am trying so hard to continue being part of this MAD world?***

-- Liz

<u>Monday, March 24, 2003</u>

"As I walk through
This wicked world
Searchin' for light in the darkness of insanity.
I ask myself
Is all hope lost?
Is there only pain and hatred, and misery?
And each time I feel like this inside,
There's one thing I wanna know:
What's so funny about peace love & understanding?

And as I walked on
Through troubled times
My spirit gets so downhearted sometimes
So where are the strong?
And who are the trusted?
And where is the harmony?
Sweet harmony."

-- Elvis Costello (of course)

<u>March 27, 2003</u>

Although I have forgiven my husband, I continue to have these recurrent night-mares. (Complete with evil agenda that resembles "The Hand That Rocks 2the

Cradle"). The theme is pretty much the same: My husband is in love with one of my closest friends. They are in love. She goes to my children's soccer games, and she takes them to the park. She talks to him intimately by phone at all hours of the day, and then goes out to bars with him at night. While I am in the hospital, she puts my children to sleep in my bed and then goes out with him. They are in love with each other. I sit and watch as she replaces me. She is healthy, energetic and sexy. I am none of those things. I am unable to intervene because of my illness, but I watch as their love unfolds, as they enjoy themselves. I cry, scream, and stamp my feet, but they don't hear me, or they pretend to not hear me. I am not sure which.

"Now, now, sweetheart - you are too sick to be ruffling your own feathers," they say as I lay in bed. Shaking their heads, they shut the bedroom door and whisper, "You better get back into bed."

But I can hear their whispers and giggles behind the closed door.

I toss, turn, sweat, and weep. I have the dream over and over. I do not wake up...

That nightmare is thankfully becoming less prevalent but it not completely gone. It is being replaced by gentler dreams full of less anxiety, angst, sadness, and grief. I even enjoy having some dreams now too, because they offer me a safe place, where I don't have to be conscious about my current waking life. And that is a welcomed respite.

Sometimes when I sense that I am waking, I will try to force the dreamlike state. It feels good to put off the inevitable grief of waking up.

I am sure it must be like that for people who are in deep grief.... Sleep provides not only a break from reality, but consolation from the inevitable deep cord of grief that is struck with wakefulness.

I don't cry, sweat, toss, or turn too much anymore. I am at peace with many of the feelings that brought me to that dark place. I remember my dreams. I take that as good sign. I am finally finding my peace.

-- Liz

<u>*March29th 2003*</u>
Thankfully another year has passed and yes, with yet another revision to my goodbye letter:

Dear Scott,

I like to think that with my transplants will come new hope and bigger, better happier love for us. I hope this is the case. I need you to know that I consider the fifteen years we've been together as a gift. I do wish the past two years could have gone differently more than anything in the world.

Our relationship is loving, caring and fun again, we share our love for food, friends, music and most of all - our beautiful children. There were plenty of funny, loving, and caring times. I feel blessed. I will choose to remember them and you positively, whether I live or die. With hopes of continued peace and love in both our futures, (and a transplant already!) Liz

April, 2003

～

*M*y Canadian transplant soul sister, Allison, got her call today for transplant!!!!!! We met a couple of years ago on a scleroderma message board on the Internet.

Our disease process is not the exactly the same, but it is similar; and eventually as we got sicker together, we also went through the process of getting listed for transplant with each other's support. Our lives have been parallel in so many ways, at so many times.

Our belief all along has been that given the nature of our relationship, it doesn't seem far-fetched to believe that our transplants will occur either one right after one another or back-to-back.

Today is her day.

Right now she is in surgery. I am thrilled for her. I cannot wait to hear from her again, and the excitement of having this day be real for at least one of us, is quite overwhelming. Please send her warm thoughts, lots of energy and healing prayers.

-- Liz

Wednesday, April 2, 2003

My friend Allison's transplant took five and a half hours. She and her two new lungs are doing well.

That is GREAT news!

-- Liz

<u>*Saturday, April 5, 2003*</u>
Today Allison is finally conscious and breathing on her own…

"Modern medicine" may get a tough rough rap sometimes…but truly this is "miracle medicine" at its best.

-- Liz

<u>*Monday, April 14, 2003*</u>
April is Organ Donation Awareness Month.

No one knows more than I do how important this is. If you are not already a donor, please consider becoming one. In many states, It is not enough to sign a donor card; you need to talk to your family about your wishes, because ultimately they will be the ones to decide whether or not to donate your organs.

It doesn't seem to make much sense does it? I mean, if you make your wishes known, you'd think that would be enough to make it happen, but that's not the case.

(As of 2006 this has changed, when New York State changed the registry from "intent" to "consent")

I believe that when a loved one dies unexpectedly, there is probably no worse time to ask someone such a deep and meaningful question. It is a time filled with grief. This loaded question of whether to donate or not is presented during this stressful grief-filled time. Really, can you make any decisions at that time? When your heart is so full of pain? I can't imagine a harder thing to do.

But somehow people are able to donate, to think of others (which really just blows me away). A friend of mine and her family thought of me specifically, when her brother-in-law passed away; they asked if there was possibility of a match in order to pass the gift of life to me. That people can think of strangers (and me specifically!) at that point in time is the truly amazing part.

But the reality is there aren't enough organs to go around. Eighty-thousand people need them. (Now in 2012, well over 115,000.) *Last year there were about 6,000 deceased donors, and 6,000 living donors…. making for a total of about 24,000 transplants.* (Remember--one person can make for many transplants.)

The math doesn't add up does it?

There needs to better way. The medical establishment is working on artificial organs and xenotransplantation (using animal organs). These things are coming, but their time has not yet arrived. Another way that is currently being discussed and debated is "presumed consent".

Presumed consent presumes that if someone dies, their organs will be made available unless the person has made their decision clear to NOT donate.--in essence, reversing the process, like you would sign a "opt- out" card -or something to that effect. Many European countries have presumed consent laws--their organ donation percentages are much higher than here in the United States.

At first I thought it seemed quite radical, and it is; but little by little it seems to make more and more sense (waiting and worrying for the past 19 months for my own transplant, I am sure, may have something to do with it.)

But in the meantime…please consider donating the gift of life to others…. it is so important.

The ultimate in recycling.

-- Liz

Wednesday, April 16, 2003
I spoke with Allison by phone this past weekend. Mostly I talked and she listened, but she was able to share with me what seems to be the toughest part of her post-transplant journey so far. "It's the psychological journey that is the toughest", she says. She admitted to me she was prepared for the physical battle --but the mental battle caught her off-guard.

Jokingly, I told her to be careful—that she could make me scared now that she knew things that I didn't from the other side (the non-waiting side).

Today, unfortunately, she is back in ICU because her lungs are collecting fluid. So PLEASE continue to keep my friend in your thoughts and prayers.

-- Liz

Wednesday April 16, 2003
Today I took a journey on the road to self-destruction--quite by accident really.

A friend of mine from high school wrote me a letter.

We haven't spoken in over 15 years. She found out about my "plight" (for lack of a better) word during an innocent Google search.

I had a really difficult time reading her letter, only because her letter was a vivid reminder of who I was--and who I now am. I am used to the person I am now; I have been this "sick" person for years now.

But her shock and anger at my disease was fresh, and took me off-guard.

I remembered a lot about who I was and who we were as teenagers, and what we wanted at that time in our lives. Hence the sadness, disappointment, anger and yes self-pity. Ugh.

-- Liz

Thursday, April 17, 2003

Time to turn up the medicine. I made the jump from 2 vials of Flolan to 3 this week. It signals time passing, it also signals increasing tolerance. I rationalize to myself that it isn't so bad. I know there are people who mix MANY more vials a day. So I still have some room.

This week I also received new pumps in the mail. More fool-proof than the old ones, I was told (emphasis on "fool").

*The nurse tutored me on my new pumps, and I found myself growing crabby, cranky and resentful. I thought, **why do I need a new pump anyway? If I am just going to get rid of it soon, right?** (I hope)... The new pumps are touted as better, but I found myself wanting to keep the old ones. I didn't want to learn a new way.... the old way was fine, I whined to myself (internally of course).*

*I listened to the nurse; she may as well have been telling me about a wonderful new invention called the automobile. Now why would I want a car when I had a horse? I marveled at my habits and resistance to change. It's such a familiar feeling to many of us (the crabbiness involved with change), and I think that for the most part I am one of the more flexible folks. I couldn't help but think, **why fix it if ain't broke?***

More importantly the reluctance to learn and accept this tool made me really realize that familiarity = comfort. You know what they say about the size of your problems, right?--they may look huge to you, but when you look in the closet to choose another one, the old one really becomes quite attractive and manageable compared to the other unfamiliar problems out there.

And THAT is what was going on with me and my new pump that day.

As I thought about it more, I realized I would probably have the same feelings once I got my new heart and lungs, even if they are perfect.

I have no doubt that I will miss my old organs and probably be even pretty cranky about it, too.

I can just hear myself now rolling my eyes and saying," My old heart never did that…"

Ahh, the realities of being human and accepting change.

-- Liz

Friday, April 25, 2003

My hero Allison is in a regular hospital room, and she is doing spectacularly - as expected. Phew.

She is walking, talking, eating, and reading.

It has been a long, tough road physically. I am afraid to ask and I think she hesitates to tell me "the skinny".

I am thankful that she is doing wonderfully.

Hooray for Allison!

-- Liz

May 2003

ᕤ

<u>Thursday, May 1, 2003</u>

In from the "Tickled Pink Department":
Allison is now home- exactly one month to the day!!!!

How is it that I can do absolutely nothing- and feel so triumphant?
How is that possible?

"Triumphant by proxy"???? (Is that legal?) I know it is possible to live vicariously through others, but is it possible to heal vicariously through others?

-- Liz

<u>Wednesday, May 7, 2003</u>

April has vanished before my very eyes. It brought lots of nice things though....
many so very normal that I could really convince myself, "I am NORMAL".

Funny, it used to be such a bad word--ugh, "normal", how utterly boring.
Now there's nothing I crave more. I beg for normalcy like a junkie begs for crack.

OK, so maybe the crack analogy is little extreme.

Recipe for Liz's Normal Month:

First, there was my daughter's birthday, (which of course lasted a good
week- as all good birthdays should). The next week brought my niece's birthday.
Then there was Easter, visiting with family, and Easter vacation (giant sigh of
relief after that was over!) A bout of strep throat followed, and the beginning
of my 7-year-old's baseball league. This weekend brings my other daughter's
communion.

Utterly normal. It makes me want to cheer. It makes want to do cartwheels.
I realize I can never be bored or think my life is dull or unexciting ever again.
Combine this with sunshine and warmth, and my spirits are soaring.

My body? Eh-eh. Not too bad, not too good. Mezzo mezzo.

My friend said to me a few weeks ago, "It's like you have split into two; your physical body and your spirit. Your spirit has got its own thing going on."

I think it really is true.

While I can sometimes be really angry at my body for not cooperating with me on this "healing thing", my mind has really, in many ways, left it behind-- searching for better.

I often have had to fight the frustration of not having a body that cooperates with all my desires. This happens every once in a while, and now is one of those times--where my spirit is a little bigger, a little stronger and more determined than my body. So while I am having a little trouble with my legs lately (I will talk more about it later). I don't care.

So there.

I was told to get a shirt that shows the score:

Liz-1

PH-0

Maybe I will....

-- Liz

<u>Monday, May 12, 2003</u>
Candy of the Week:
    Life Saver Kickerz
    Yum yum!
    -- Liz

<u>Tuesday, May 13, 2003</u>
To prepare for her communion, Luci had to attend class outside her regular religious education class. (In 4th grade, she is older than most kids participating, finally getting around to it, just another parental duty to feel guilty about). I took her to class one night. There were about 3 or 4 kids in the class. The teacher asked to start class with a prayer and asked for the children's intentions. I stood out in the hallway, eavesdropping.

The first child asked for Jesus to help to his friend, the next wanted to pray for her mother, who was having some type of surgery the next day.

Then the teacher asked Luci what she wanted to pray for. She said without hesitation. 'Derek Jeter' (New York Yankee shortstop). The teacher repeated, "Derek Jeter?"

Luci explained. "He hurt his arm - he is going to be out for a whole month."

I could tell this was a serious matter from her tone of voice. I laughed and put my hand over my mouth. I was still standing in the hallway. I thought, **Hey! Derek Jeter has more juice than I, her own mother, who needs a transplant.** *I don't even rank with my own kid.*

Later as Derek Jeter began to heal, she took credit for it, too. "Look mom, I made Derek Jeter better with my prayers."

In the end, I did make the final cut. My daughter included my future transplants and me in her prayer intention that she read during the actual communion mass. And what of Luci and Derek Jeter? She got a baseball autographed by Derek Jeter from her uncle as a communion gift.

-- Liz

<u>*Monday, May 19, 2003*</u>

Talking about my spirits brings me to talking about my death… you say "Ah… how did this conversation take a turn for the worse?"

Ultimately death is the final split between your mind, spirit, soul (take your pick), and body.

I was 16 when I realized that I was not afraid of death.

I have always enjoyed my life, and even at that young age I thought **if this is "it" then this would be good enough for me. If I died today, I thought, I would be satisfied with the life I have lived up until now.**

I thought that question would always be the benchmark for how I lived my life. **Liz, if you died today, would that be enough?**

I would check in with myself obsessively (as only a teenager can):

If I died today, would I be ok with that?

I realized as time passed, that the answer more often than not was "yes". Except of course for the few adolescent tragedies that made me wish I were dead. (You know, breaking up with my boyfriend, arguing with my girlfriend, living with a huge pimple that me and all my friend's nicknamed Mt Vesuvius….things like that.)

If I died today, would I be ok with it?
If I died today, would I be ok with it?
*Conclusion: **Life had been good enough**, I thought. I was ok with it.*
There was nothing "I had to do".
I decided death was ok. I could accept if I needed to.

Little did I know that it wouldn't be that easy, and that I am not so big bad and powerful to have any kind of power over death…ah but I was young and invincible.

No, I am still not so attached to this body I call my own. But my desire and will to live is impossible to express.

The difference is simple. That difference is the girls.

*For the first time in my life I find myself saying **I DON'T WANT TO DIE.** I want to live and do my job as a mother to the best of my abilities.*

All of a sudden I find myself in a completely different position. I am stamping my feet and digging them in the dirt as this nasty thing pulls me away from all I know and want.

I have been to that terrible place. Crying and muttering from my bed, I have begged God to let me live, and in the same breath; I have begged him to let me die.

I know my body is only a temporary vehicle (and it certainly ain't no five star hotel!), but the only truly important part of me--my spirit-- is happy to have the accommodations…for now.

-- Liz

<u>Tuesday, May 20, 2003</u>
> *"What keeps you going isn't some fine destination but just the road you're on, and the fact that you know how to drive."*
> *-- Barbara Kingsolver*

<u>Friday, May 23, 2003</u>
My transplant center has not done one heart / lung combo yet this year, which is not so strange since they typically only do 1 or 2 per year. But they have done no lungs of my blood type at all, which is very strange.

Generally they do about 50 lung transplants per year. This year they have only done approximately 15 in the first 6 months of this year, which is well behind their usual average.

What's it all mean? I don't know.

Perhaps it means that my time will come soon. Or maybe it means I will be watching another winter roll in right before my very eyes. Who Knows...

YUCK

I can't take it anymore.

-- Liz

June, 2003

❧

47 Degrees and pouring rain.

Not exactly ideal weather conditions for a "Walk in the park", but over 200 folks braved the yucky weather for the first National Scleroderma Foundation walk here locally.

I was blown away to see that many people brave the elements. As one friend of mine put it, "Hey, not only did I walk in the freezing cold and rain, but I also paid to do it." Not many people would do that…no, not many would.

But many people did. And Oh yes…. the Pfizer (maker of Viagra) drug representative introduced herself to me at the walk. She was a lovely lady who told me that she reads my journal regularly.

And with that, my already "small world" became even a little bit smaller…

…but I am smiling with glee.

Happy shiny (wet and cold) people laughing: 1

Evil disease extraordinaire: 0

-- Liz

Tuesday, June 3, 2003

Yesterday was my daughter's birthday. Luci turned 10! Hooray!

You know of course what she can't say right? ("My Mom Died when I was nine years old") Ha! I feel triumphant, joyous and blessed to have celebrated another year.

A few days ago, I realized that the anniversary of my illness passed without me even noticing. That MUST be a good sign. Three years have passed. Thirty-six months of I-feel-like-complete-and-utter-shit. It feels like both forever and nothing at the same time.

I saw my diplomas in passing the other day in the basement. There they were, covered with dust and cobwebs, lying in a box in the dark corner of my basement. I paused when I saw them. They took me by surprise. I reflected upon their old, dusty and relic look. They are only 4 years old.

I closed the box and headed back upstairs. Maybe one day they will be important to me again, I thought.

And then again maybe they won't. I am ok with that.

It was important to me then; not so much now. I have learned that you never know what you can expect from life...or what is truly important.

-- Liz DeVivo MA, LMSW

(What the heck I paid for them. I might as well use 'em cause I got 'em)

Wednesday, June 4, 2003

The figures are in for the Scleroderma Foundation walk-a-thon. Our wonderful community donated approximately $20,000 to fund continuing support and research at the Foundation. That is wonderful!

Of the four walks in the Tri-State Area (walks in Long Island, Connecticut, New Jersey, and Binghamton, New York); Binghamton came in second only to Long Island. That says a lot about the lovely community we live in, even if the sun doesn't shine. Who needs sunny and warm?

It's the people, not the weather that keep me warm here.

-- Liz

Monday, June 9, 2003

Our cat Pooh is missing. He has been missing for a few weeks. I keep holding out hope that someone would find him and return him to us. But no such luck. It has been heartbreaking for us. He is the long-awaited kitten we got last fall. I mean, he was in our family Christmas picture and everything.

We searched the neighborhood; the animal shelters, the roads, and the shoulder of roads. Nothing. We went door to door asking neighbors.

Some sighted him, and so we held on to some hope for a time.

Finally, "The Pooh is never going to come back, is he Mom?" -reality is hitting us all.

Scott was initially pretty angry about the whole situation, mostly because he was powerless in terms of helping the girls with their grief and sorrow.

He said to me one night as we were eating dinner, "You know Liz, I hate telling them. I don't know what's going to happen, whether we will find the cat or not. Not knowing what to say to them to make their pain better reminds of when you were in the hospital…" His voice trailed off.

I put my hand up in the classic don't go there pose. I said, in my best "let me make myself clear" voice, "Don't you dare tell me you are comparing the cat's disappearance to me dying, ok?"

He laughed and put his hand on my shoulder in an effort to relax me. I shot him the evil eye, and then laughed, too.

How did life become so ridiculous?

Oh poor Pooh…

-- Liz

<u>*Monday, June 16, 2003*</u>

Summer vacation plans and the thought of the continued wait.

It is that time of the year again--time to make plans for summer. Time to sign everyone up for the things they want to do in hopes of surviving the summer--I can't believe that I am doing it again. I really thought I would have different plans this summer because I would be all healed up and ready to go. We have talked about what we will do if the call comes during the summer, most likely we will take the kids to Pittsburgh and find a place while I heal. Or, if it's during school year they will stay here…who know? It just depends on a lot of things; I know I can't bear being away from my girls any longer than I have to.

Some days pass with few thoughts of a call. Mostly my anxiety is directly correlated to how I feel. If I feel pretty well, then I feel invincible, and I busy myself with fantasies of miraculous healing. Then there are the days when I suffer, and I feel like my heart is going burst, I scare myself with fantasies from the darker side.

And there are darker days when I suffer with the feeling of my hair standing up on the back of my neck for no reason at all. Those are the days that really get me going, because my feelings are based on absolutely nothing at all. Some days I feel intuitive, and I think, this is The Day. Most days I feel nothing, and let it go at that.

I have been waiting 22 months. Ugh. It took 15 months for the first call….
Now serving psychological torture samples in aisle 5…
-- Liz

My illness of course took its toll on my girls. The girls dealt with my illness like the two different people they are. Emma was more willing to look, ask questions and talk in general about what was happening. Luci didn't want to speak about it at all, was happy to be close to me, but never on my right side (as that was where my catheter site was). So the standard set up for snuggling in bed, was Luci on the left and Emma on the right, until I had to have the catheter replaced multiple times, and then that confused everything and everyone for some time, lots of jumping around and switching sides in bed. Luci was not comfortable with anything medical; she had a very hard time when I was hospitalized, sometime not even wanting to come in the room, lingering at the door playing her Nintendo DS. Emma would just jump into the hospital bed and snuggle up. They were different children, who handled things differently. And make no mistake--it was very hard on each of them. They asked very tough questions at times, and it pained me to answer their questions. I was always torn, never quite certain about how much information I wanted to share with them, yet knowing I needed to prepare them for my death. It was torturous for me at times to try to figure out what to share and what to withhold--with each of them--because they each had different levels of what they could tolerate talking about.

I remember reading them The Kissing Hand, a beautiful children's book that talks about separation; which was perfect because we often talked about being separated, either short term (like when I was hospitalized), and long term as in--gulp--forever. Other moms read The Kissing Hand to their children on the first day of school to help ease their separation anxiety. Oh, how I envied those moms.

The book came with stickers to help remind children that their parent/loved one was always with them even when they were not present. We each took a sticker to help remind us. I had my own sticker that I stuck to my Flolan pump to help me remember the same thing. The girls stuck there stickers on their bed, their toys, wherever; eventually I had to make my own stickers because we ran out of the ones that came with the book.

The conversations we had were never easy, but basically held the same message. "No matter where I am, I will always be with you. Right?" and they would nod there sweet little heads and I would quiz them: "Where will I be?"--and they would point to their hearts and their heads. It was the best I could do. We also talked about heaven, and what beautiful place heaven was.

The first year I was sick, our conversations were mostly centered around what I thought was inevitable--my death. But after I was listed for a transplant, things became more hopeful. We started fantasizing about all the fun things I would be able to do with them when I was transplanted. We talked about how I would walk them to the park (which was literally down the street about 250 ft.; yet I still had to drive to it, because we lived slightly uphill of the park which made it impossible for me to walk). We talked about how I would be able to pick them up, as in literally--something I hadn't been able to do for many years now. (Good God, I could barely hold my 8-pound niece when she was born!) My kids had not been picked up or held by me in many years. We had created a "pretend hold me" which was when the kids needed to be hugged and held they would climb up on the kitchen counter and then wrap their legs and arms around me so I could hold them and comfort them and pretend to carry them.

We talked about how I would take them to the park, run after them; how we would walk to school and get a dog to take care of and walk on our own…all these seemingly mundane fantasies are what kept us all going. Of that I have no doubt.

My kids were young and had to responsible for many things other kids were not. Each morning they dressed themselves before school and I would just have them jump on my bed, before they left so I could "officially approve" their outfit. Most days were "anything goes"…every once in a while I had to veto an outfit mostly because of climate issues. (No, you cannot wear shorts Luci, it's February and there is a foot of snow outside.)

I would serve them breakfast. Most meals were served in paper plates as I did not have the strength to load and unload the dishwasher. I learned quickly it was depressing to see the dishes pile up and not be able to take care of them. I could have had the girls do them, but I felt that they were responsible for enough. So at times, it was hard to decide what a normal age-appropriate chore was and what wasn't. Because we lived close to the school they were walkers, and sometimes I simply could not get out of bed or drive; they would have to walk. They were in kindergarten and second grade. It was tortuous for me to send them out the door. The school insisted there hands were tied as I lived less than a ½ mile from school and they could not make an exception for my girls. The school's secretary, however, would call me to let me know when they had arrived which was always a welcome relief. It didn't take long before I set them up with "day-care" at my neighbor's house, whose house was thankfully on the bus route and literally 75 feet away thru my backyard.

When the girls came home from school through the backyard and back door, they would shout their arrival, "Mom we are home!" I would answer (from my bed) and they would usually get their own snack out of the fridge, and then come to my bedroom to show me their school work, eat their snack in my bed and just talk about their day.

What I didn't know until many years later, was that Luci would scream every time she came in the door not because she was a loud kid, which is what I always chalked it up to, but because she was afraid I wouldn't reply. Every day when she came home from school, she was afraid to come home and find me dead. It would take her many years to admit that to me. That poor child. I had no idea. We were just trying to do the best job we could, given the circumstances.....So while other families had simple rules like "don't eat on the couch", or "do your homework before TV"... we just didn't. We were just trying to hang on.

Their grandfather came over most days after school to sit with them and help them do their homework, and this would help bridge the gap until their father came home from work. And that's how we survived some of the worst days, weeks, months, and years of my illness.

In a few years the girls would remember little about my illness. They are (not surprisingly) very resilient. My illness took a toll on them; of that I have no doubt.

But it wasn't long before they became demanding teenagers, asking me take them to the mall, their friends' houses, and the movies, as if nothing ever happened.

Wednesday, June 18, 2003
I remembered this week a moment in time that I hadn't thought about before. Remember I said the luxury/curse of health is the ability to actually think about and remember things? And how forgetting is the body's lovely way of surviving? (Let's have a big cheer for memory loss and denial- Hip hip hooray!)

I remembered being in the hospital. My girlfriend Irene was with me. When the doctor came in, he asked for privacy and drew the curtain.

When he was done, I realized that she hadn't come back. I said, "Irene? Irene? Where are you?"

There she was behind the curtain, which was still drawn around my bed. I knew she was there --I could see her feet. Her feet were shuffling around, like she was doing the pee pee dance. Only she wasn't. She was crying. I could hear the sniffles and grunts. At which point I said, "What are you doing?"

She answered back sheepishly, with the shame of a kid who had been busted doing something wrong. "Crying".

I opened the curtain, and we cried together.

Now I remind myself continually, Pull up the curtain--there is no need to hide in pain.

It's so much easier that way.
-- Liz

Friday, June 20, 2003
I made my appointment for my yearly evaluation in for August.

I can't believe it's that time again. I said as much to my transplant coordinator. She couldn't believe it either and added, "Don't worry--I make these appointments all the time, and people get called soon after." Oh don't I wish…

In the meantime, I have an appointment with my pulmonary hypertension specialist in New York City next week. I am getting prepared--emotionally. Seems that I always crash and burn after seeing my doctors (gee Liz, you think so??) It's a terrible habit I am trying to break.

But it won't be all work and no play. We have fun things planned for the girls.
-- Liz

July, 2003

～

I have been thoroughly enjoying summer with my friends and family. But today is one of those days where I wish my phone would ring. I am tired and very aware of my body, the pounding in my chest, the aches in my legs, arms, and head.

It's not every day that I make that wish. Some days I feel so good and full of energy that I am left feeling confused by my body. Mostly I get just get downright tired of my very high-maintenance body. And that won't change with transplants, either. The high-maintenance part, that is…the constant taking care of myself.

Besides the daily care (changing pumps, mixing medicine, and taking medicine), there is the simple fact that I can't do anything without intensive preparation.

Each day I check my beeper to make sure the batteries are not low, and make sure that it is even on. I charge and carry my cell phone, and always make sure someone knows where I am at all times--especially when I am out of range.

I make arrangements with air pilots wherever I go--just in case. So if go to a soccer tournament, I have a pilot on standby. If I visit my mother I have pilot. If I take the kids to Sesame Place (which we just did last week), I notify my transplant coordinators and have a pilot on call-- just in case.

Oh how very nice it would be to just walk out of my house and not have to make a single arrangement, not have to pack large grocery bags worth of medicine, and not care if I have enough ice packs to make through the day…

I am sorry; I know I am whining now.

Who I am to complain? I chastise myself. I am lucky, blessed, and eternally grateful for the opportunity to do such things. I am outrageously stubborn with my independence--it is both my strength and my greatest weakness.

My mother's favorite descriptive term to use in reference of me is terca. Terca is a Spanish word that is close in meaning to stubborn; but it also can refer to an animal such as a bull.

Really, that is how I continue to on this journey. Terca. Stubborn like bull.

-- Liz

Wednesday, July 9, 2003

Today I decided that I was born in the wrong century. I should have had this disease say a century ago in …China. I should have been a queen, or princess, or the head of a great house a century ago in China.

At the very least, I would receive constant attention. I would be cared for at all times by one of my many servants from the comfort of my luxurious velvet chaise lounge. I would be cooked for, fed, bathed, and dressed without ever missing a heartbeat (get it? Oh I am killing myself here!)

Anyway, in my dream life of privilege, I would never exert myself physically--I would never huff and puff and want to throw up.

Oh, I could survive this disease if I had to do absolutely nothing to do but sit and point from my velvet chaise lounge…

The irony of course, is that I own a chaise lounge, and if you ask anyone who has seen me pointing and grunting from my chaise/ throne (in particular my husband), they'd all tell you that I don't need to go back a hundred years…

-- Liz

Friday, July 18, 2003

There's a lot of freedom in being healthy. Never take it for granted. I am a slave to my health now, and I always will be. (Now with pumps, later with a lifetime of immunosuppressants.) I can't help but think about it, sometimes with even a little bit of resentment. What I wouldn't give to function with never having to give my body a second thought.

*I think about people with lifelong illnesses. How hard it must be to cope day in and day out…for a **lifetime.** I have "only" been sick for 3 out of my 36 years. (Talk about perspective!)*

*My journey is very confusing. I don't know which direction I am heading in, or supposed to heading in. I ask for guidance and patience regularly. **Please God,***

I pray, *help me see where I am supposed to go, what choices I should make for my body, and what choices I should let others make.*

*As I said--confused. Do I **choose** a road? Or do I just let myself be led down a road. Just how "in charge" of me am I really? Am I fooling myself thinking that I have that much power, control, and say to make choices? Who is in charge of this life of mine?*

A feminist would say I am in charge of my destiny. A scientist would say that doctors, research, and science are in charge.

*The spiritual would say that God is in control. I am learning **that my journey** is a combination of all three of us-- me, my doctors, and God. And I am glad to not be alone.*

-- Liz

<u>*Saturday July 19, 2003*</u>
You know what they say: There are no accidents. The hand of Fate, or God, has determined our fate/ future.

I really believe that there are no coincidences. It all happens for a reason, and I would be the first to tell you that I spend a lot of time assigning meaning to events and moments in my life.

Take for instance that fact that I worked with people who were dying before I got sick…that is no coincidence for sure.

I made the decision to work with HIV/AIDS patients simply because the position was part time. I wanted part time hours so I could be home with the girls.

It was a difficult decision because I struggled with the idea of working with people who were dying I knew that this area of work – death and dying -was not my forte. I knew it would be difficult work.

My area of expertise professionally was in family crisis and violence. I had worked in family crisis and violence for over 10 years. I remembered working once with a family who toddler was dying of cancer. The family was referred to the program not for the child or for the grief, but for the other children in the family who knew no other ways to cope but with violence. They were violent with each other, and with other people in school and within their community.

I worked with a hospice worker for the first time there. She admired what I did (I don't know how you do it). And I admired what she did (I could never do what you are doing). We agreed to be there at the family's home together.

I needed her; I was scared to be in that house alone if the baby died. She needed me. She was scared to be in the house for one of the many violent interactions between family members.

I learned a lot during that time about death and myself. Mostly, I learned that I could not really deal with "it". By the time I was done working with that family, I had an uncontrollable eye twitch that a week's vacation in Puerto Rico couldn't cure.

Bottom line was I knew that grief was not my professional forte professionally. But somehow, someway, I accepted that position working with HIV/AIDs patients…and I learned so much.

I was witness to incredible spiritual strength. Most days I was awed by the things I learned, about people, suffering and true joy.

I only worked there 6 months, before I became ill. But I was fortunate to witness others live with dignity, with priorities, and a sense of what truly matters in their lifetime.

That's no accident. (I am sure you will agree)
-- Liz

<u>Sunday July 20, 2003</u>
Last week I had the good fortune and health to go on a family beach vacation. YEAH for New Jersey beaches!

Monday I head to New York City for a cardiac MRI…BOO!
-- Liz

<u>Tuesday, July 29, 2003</u>
I was going to write about how my transplant Internet buddy Allison is visiting me this weekend.

Then I was going to write about the MRI I had and how shitty I feel.
Instead I am saying its 4:45 am and
I got the call
I GOT the call
I got THE call
I got the CALL
But more importantly, I HAVE A PLANE!!!!!! (And a pilot)
I am at peace and thrilled.

We are leaving shortly I need to be at the hospital by 8:45.

I hope this is the real thing and not another false alarm. Please pray with me.

-- Liz

<u>*Tuesday, July 29, 2003*</u>

"Blackbird singing in the dead of night
Take these broken wings and learn to fly
All your life
You were only waiting for this moment to arise.

Blackbird singing in the dead of night
Take these sunken eyes and learn to see
All your life
You were only waiting for this moment to be free..."
-- The Beatles

The girls on our beach vacation the week before my call.

This is the picture that gave me the strength to hang on.
I had a huge copy of it hung on the wall (poster sized!) in
my hospital room during my painfully long stay.

November 2003

November 26, 2003
I am Home.
 I am Home!
I am HOME!!!
I AM HOME!!!!!!

December 2003

December 12, 2003

I have been unable to write for a long time now. I apologize. At first I understood why I wasn't able to write. My eyesight was blurry from all the medicine; I could not make out words on the screen. My tremors, also from the medicine, kept me away from pecking away at the keys. The simple act of sitting up in a chair was an intense physical chore. It made sense to me why I would be unable to write then. Then time passed and many of the most intense side effects went away. But I was still unable to write. However, the light bulb in my brain went on this morning; I understand now why I haven't been able to write: it's because I am overwhelmed. At first it was physically. Now I understand that I am emotionally overwhelmed.

Just from all I have been through, all I am going through.

It's about all that I've suffered and all I have learned and gained. It's about pain and joy.

It's overwhelming. All of it.

Where do I start...with the pain or the joy? I don't seem to know. It seems important to express the hardest journey of my life, but at the same time there are so many feelings I am unable to explain. In a strange way it reminds me slightly of childbirth, An event that is horrendously painful but as soon as you see the baby, it almost doesn't seem to matter. Nature's lovely way of ensuring that we keep having children, right? Forget the pain. Block the pain, or, do as I did--have a good old-fashioned psychotic breakdown. Medical or "PC" term: ICU medically induced psychosis. My poor mother said, "She got new lungs and heart but she lost her mind instead".

I love that one. (Like it was a tradeoff...)

*I have regained my senses (for the most part), and have been putting it all behind me since then. Reminding myself over and over, **forget the labor; it's the baby that matters now.***

-- Liz

January 2004

<u>*January 21, 2004*</u>
Last week I went to Pittsburgh for a bronchoscopy and biopsy. In general, my heart and lungs checked out ok, but a few days after returning home I was told that I have a lung infection called Nocardia. I have been started on oral and IV antibiotics. I don't feel really well, and I am not sure if it's the treatment (antibiotics) or the actual sickness that keeps me queasy. At any rate, it's not stopping me and my family from going to Florida this next week. Perhaps some sunny and warm weather will help.

Scott surprised the girls and me by planning the trip. It just happens to be our 11th anniversary, so we will be celebrating that, too. Now I just have to feel better so I can enjoy myself.

I am sure both my PICC line and I are up to the task.

-- Liz

February 2004

February 4, 2004

*We are back from warm and sunny Florida. It was good for my body and good for my soul. I was able to walk down to the beach with my kids, which was quite the accomplishment. It was the first time since the transplant that I felt "dare I say", **triumphant** over my disease. And where usually you'd find me in a wheelchair, I walked instead. Now don't get me wrong, I still used the wheelchair (for Sea World), but I didn't need it the whole time. When I got out of breath, that was it, I was just out of breath; I wasn't in any kind of pain. What an amazing treat!*

*It felt good. **Really good.***

It confirmed for me that I am FINALLY really starting to feel better...
Hurray!

This trip was the first indication that things were changing for me. My entire world shifted that day and the black hole lifted; I realized for the first time that things had truly changed for me. This was information that I hadn't known for sure until then: **I was getting better.** Some people know this immediately after their transplant. My only indication after transplant that anything was different was that my lips were pink instead of blue. It took me 6 months to really know that I all I went through was not in vain. From then on, each day I got better and better, emotionally and physically.

The joy had sneaked its way into me, and was now expanding.

-- *Liz*

February 5, 2004

> *"Every tomorrow has two handles. We can take hold of it with the handle of anxiety or the handle of faith."*
> *-- HENRY WARD BEECHER*

I have been having some trouble lately with guilt from my transplant. Survivor's guilt. Now, I thought I knew everything I needed to know about this phenomenon, so I thought I would be ready for it. I underestimated its scope and magnitude. Not only is there the guilt I have for my donor--**Why is it that I got to live and she got to die?--but there's also, Why do I get to live when there are so many others with this disease that only get to suffer and die?**

How come I am so lucky and blessed? How did that happen? I will never know the answer.

But I know that I will use my gift everyday with great awe, and live life to its fullest.

I reason with myself, that my donor gave me life. Life is the only good thing that can happen from a tragic death. What a gift it is to give life in the end.

But why me? And why her? And why not others?

I imagine it will just take time....sigh.

-- Liz

March 2004

<u>*March 23, 2004*</u>
Yesterday I fell down the stairs and broke my foot--in three places. I am starting to think that my mission in life is to meet every doctor of every type specialty in the triple cities.

It hurts, but not horrifically, I am even able to laugh at myself. **It's not really too bad,** *I console myself. Besides, this injury is a real treat--it's actually something that will heal all on its own, imagine that! That is something I am not too familiar with nor used to. It is quite thrilling to know that one's body can get better on its own.*

Besides, something had to slow me down enough so I could take the time to write in my journal. I do feel as though I have a lot to say, and never enough time to write about it. So perhaps this is a good thing.

However, falling down the steps in front of my girls, my friend, and my husband was not a good thing. The girls were re-traumatized when I fell, and they spent the next few minutes crying and sobbing. We reassured them I was alright (although I wanted to cry and sob right along with them); and later when I asked them what they were thinking when I fell, Emma did not skip a beat when she answered, "death".

Poor child. *How much they have suffered. Fortunately, overall, I think they have done an excellent job coping with me, my illness, and travails.*

So now you can put scissors, knives, and STAIRS on my list of things I need to stay away from.

-- Liz

<u>*March 28, 2004*</u>
I had the honor and the privilege of seeing my nephew born a few weeks ago. His name is Joseph and he was born at 25 weeks. He is tiny and fragile, weighing a whopping 1lb 14oz. (he is now 2 pounds 2 oz.)

When my-sister-in-law told me she was in labor, I made the trip to New York to be with her and my brother. It was important to all of us.

It was important for me to be there since I was unable to participate in the previous birth of my niece, 3 years ago. As a matter of fact, I was so ill at that point in time that I was not even able to hold my niece. She was too heavy for me to carry, even though she was just a newborn.

For Nicole (my sister-in-law), it was important that I be there, because as a person lucky enough to have a miracle happen in my life, perhaps I could bring some "miracle mojo" to her and her son.

I like to think that perhaps the miracle that worked its way into my life has been shared with baby Joseph and his oh-so-fragile, but lovely life. Knowing that my family has been blessed with 2 miracles in one year is not something that will be ignored by any of us at home anytime soon. We have been blessed--twice. How wonderful.

Please keep him in your prayers.

-- Liz

April 2004

I have had a busy couple of weeks with the girls being home for spring vacation. Busy with lovely milestones big and small.

I took the girls to New York for Easter (big milestone) drove all by myself! We visited people--instead of people visiting us!

I made the move from medical physical rehab, to the regular gym (hooray!)

And last but not least, we moved our bedroom downstairs, where it's supposed to be, because P.T., i.e., pretransplant I could not climb the stairs. So we had it on the second level of the house. I was very attached to it, loved it there and loved the view out the window, but it was time for the change. Besides, even though I love the view, there were many dark and trying times lying in that room. So it was a good goodbye.

Now the girls have their own rooms and they are thrilled about it, and I still nap up there on occasion.

-- Liz

April 23, 2004

When I was in the hospital, I trembled much of the time--either I was sick and trembling, cold and trembling, or just trembling from the medication. I had a visualization/hallucination (meaning it was partly deliberate and partly delivered) while I was in the hospital that helped me get through these moments of suffering. Thinking back on it now, I know it helped me a great deal.

When I would begin to tremble and shake (or get the chills), I would imagine angels, thousands of them, in the shape of small golden fireflies, landing on my body--creating a bright and golden blanket to protect me from feeling badly. In my mind, I knew that each angel or firefly was a friend or stranger praying for me. Somehow knowing this made the suffering a little easier to tolerate. And I would find comfort.

I would then welcome the chills as a sign of angels visiting me (a soothing alternative to the dread).

-- Liz

<u>*April 27, 2004*</u>

I am wearing two shoes again--hurray!

Now it's time to find a dance class....maybe belly dancing?

-- Liz

<u>*April 29, 2004*</u>

Ode to the PICC Line.

Oh happy day! Today my nurse told me that I could finally get off the IV anti-biotics I have been on since January. HURRAY! I am so thrilled. The darn thing had irritated my arm to the point of bleeding. The nurse came a few minutes ago and pulled all 16 or so inches of it out of me. HA.

The PICC line is gone; I am officially cord-free (for now anyway)!

That's two liberating events in one week…WOW! I am feeling pretty lucky; watch out!

-- Liz

May 2004

<u>May 7, 2004</u>
The end of May will mark another major milestone for me in my healing journey: This month my handicapped status expires. May 31.

I dreaded that day from the moment I was "given" my handicapped status, and the parking privileges that come with it. At that time, I never believed I would live to see the day. It was a day long ago that ended with me in tears, fearful that I would "expire" before my parking tag.

Somehow, someway, I have beaten the race against my handicapped parking tag.

I was right about one thing however. I won't see the tag renewed--but not for the reasons I originally thought.

Three years back when I would think about May 2004, I would think of it in fear. No doctor said I would even make it that far, so I never really considered that the feeling I could be feeling instead of fearful was triumphant (and humble always humble).

And nowadays, when I'm feeling big bad and triumphant, I know that the reality is that I could be standing in line for the damn tag again next month--so as I said, the key word here is humble--ever so humble, grateful and appreciative.

And another lesson is learned: that the dreaded event unraveled into a moment of triumph and humility--something I never expected to happen that way. But I should know by now (you'd think), that expecting the unexpected is the unwritten rule of (my) life. (Talk to me later when I am huffing and puffing my way from parking lot XYZ...)

The other lesson is, "never believe what the doctors say". They may know a lot and be very smart--but they don't know everything. And more importantly, they can never admit they may not know everything (because of course you know, they would be held liable if they made this admission). WOW--does that make sense? Of course it does.

But I know my doctors are just as happy and thrilled as I am that they were wrong.

-- Liz

<u>*May 11, 2004*</u>
This weekend was Emma's Communion. The family spent time together eating and playing. We went swimming (my first time in water in about 4 years!), and then I jumped on a trampoline with my girls.

How fun is that?

This morning I am going to walk my girls to school. I set that goal a very long time ago.

Once, a reporter for the local newspaper asked me the question, "What do you look forward to doing after your transplant?"

My response was, "I want to walk my kids to school."

Today is the day, and the reporter is here to do a follow up story.

Post Script:

The Scene: The Living Room
Me: Guess what?
Girls (no answer, watching TV).
Me: (excited) Today I want to walk to school with you!
Girls (no answer, still watching TV).
Me: Come on girls, let's get going. Time to go to school…
Girls: Mom, we don't want to walk. Can't you just drive us?
Me: (trying to stay positive) No, it's a beautiful day; we need to get going if we are going to make it to school on time.
Girls: (full, all-out whining) But MOM, we want to see the rest of the show!
Liz: (grabs the remote, turns the TV off, and growls) It's time to walk to school. NOW! And you're GONNA like it. Let's go!
(Ok maybe it wasn't that bad…but close.)

What is up with these children? I could tell them we were going to Disney World or the dentist for multiple tooth extractions and I'd get the same reaction out of them.

What is up with that?
-- Liz

Photo Courtesy of Press and Sun Bulletin

<u>May 27, 2004</u>

> *"Faith is not a belief, nor is it based on reason. Faith is a*
> *choice we make to enter into things as they are and to work*
> *with and learn from whatever is happening, no matter*
> *how impossible it may seem. It is a choice we make to open*
> *ourselves to possibilities that are unseen and unknown."*
> *-RICHARD AND ANTRA BOROFSKY*

I have attended a healing Mass regularly for the past few years. It has really helped me to hold on, when otherwise I may have let go. The priest that held these healing Masses said each and every time, "Don't ask for a miracle--expect a miracle." That was, and still is, very powerful to me.

I really enjoy this Mass and feel that I have received many gifts by attending. However my mistaken assumption all along has been that it is helpful and healing to me. It never really occurred to me that I could be giving some faith, peace, and healing to someone else.

I had this little construct of mine challenged recently, when I was sitting in church and someone brought their toddler to me, and asked if I would pray for her.

Immediately I felt foolish. Who am I? I thought. I am not a healer; that's not my job. I rationalized: If I knew how to heal, then I wouldn't be in the mess I am in, right? What use could I be to this child and her mother?

But without hesitation, that mother handed me her child, so I held her. She explained that since a miracle had worked its way through my life already, that I was a conduit for miracles; perhaps it could happen for her daughter.

I looked in the child's eyes, she looked right back at me. She was perfectly comfortable with me, a stranger, holding her.

So I prayed. And when it was over, I smiled at the girl and she smiled back. I handed her back to her mother.

And for as awkward of a moment as it was for me, it was filled with amazement and gigantic size awe for the faith that some people are so blessed to have.

It blew me away.

-- Liz

July 2004

～

*A*h... *I think it is time to write about the transplant. Actually, it's time to write about many things.*

My new Birthday (anniversary of my transplant) is coming up at the end of this month, and while I am very excited about it, I feel that I have some personal goals to which I have not yet attended, and now need to. One of those (many) things is writing about the transplant.

I am not sure if I am ready to start writing, but I know that I no longer want to entertain the memories that float through and around my brain. Sometimes the visit is short, other times the visit is overstayed. Writing about it is a definite chore that I have been trying to accomplish for some time now.

But there is something about reliving that hell that is, well, unappealing to say the least. But I know and understand that the event needs to be remembered for what it was, so that I can move on. I think I will divide the event into 4 parts, for both simplicity's sake and my own sanity.

The Call, in and of itself, is worthy of its own part. Then, the hospital stay in 3 parts: the first 6 weeks, the second 6 weeks, and the third 6 weeks.

So perhaps by dividing it up by time, I will be able to make sense of the life-changing event that exists only in small threads in my head.

My first clue, other than what I remember, is to look back at the journal and read what Scott wrote to everyone in order to keep them updated while I was in the hospital. I have read through it twice, and asked a lot of questions before really having even a small understanding of what happened; I still don't have much of a handle on it.

(Incidentally, I told Scott he minimized my horrific experience; he agreed, and said he was trying his best to not only stay positive, but to keep people from panicking when they read his updates.)

For my next clue, I requested copies of my medical records to help with remembering the more concrete facts.

Finally, I relied on letters and emails sent to me during that time, and also on conversations with family members, because they have helped me to remember from an emotional perspective.

Here's my stab at it….A little transplant humor before we dive into the abyss.
-- Liz

<u>*July 5, 2004*</u>
I don't remember a thing about the day before my call. I think it was just a regular Monday, until sometime early Tuesday morning. It was around 4:40 a.m. or so, when we were awakened by the sound of one of the girls' toys--you know how when the battery dies in a toy, it sometimes goes haywire?

Well, this is what happened that morning: the girls' toy Target cash register just started in with its chanting: **Ding-ding, Credit Approved! ding-ding, Credit Approved!, ding-ding…**

…over and over. Every once in a while it would sneak a **"Thank you for shopping at Target!"** *in, but mostly it just kept repeating,* **"Credit approved!"**

Little did I know that my Karmic credit was literally and truly being approved **right at that very moment.**

I had just sent Scott to the living room where he was busy taking a kitchen knife to the register when the phone began ringing.

He stopped beating on it; it stopped chanting, and I picked up the phone knowing exactly who was in the other end.

I answered it (very) awake, happily and at peace, not many people answer a call at 4:45 am in this manner. My transplant coordinator said, "Liz this is your call; we are offering you a new set of heart and lungs today. Will you accept them?" (This sounds like a ridiculous question I know, but it is official transplant etiquette).

I said something--I don't know really what--to the effect of, "Oh my God. It's finally my day…" I accepted the offer and told her I would be there as soon as possible.

I then began the phone calls; to the pilots, to my father-in-law, whom I informed at that moment to pack his bag and join us. I then called my family, so they could begin their trip to Pittsburgh as well; and then lastly the neighbors, to take us up to the airport and to stay with the girls.

All of this came easily, and I was excited and at peace all at the same time…

…until it was time to go, it was now 6 am and our flight was leaving at 7am. I realized that I had a choice to make; wake up the girls and tell them I was going, or not?

I walked up to their bedroom with every intention of telling them the good news, and then I felt the fear and dread sink in. What if they were scared--and worse-- what if I was saying goodbye to them for good? Forever? I had always prayed and begged God to let me stay alive for their sake; in my head the magic number was 47. I wanted eleven more years. I wanted to stay alive at least till I was 47 years old—so I could at least get them through high school and Emma to 18 years old. This transplant was the only hope I had to get to that magic number.

I couldn't even begin to grasp the enormity of the situation before me.

I couldn't do it. I couldn't wake them.

So I let them be.

I stared at them in their sleep, and blew them each a kiss; and then I ran down the stairs, crying.

I think those were the only tears I shed that day.

It was a beautiful day. The flight was about 40 minutes long on a plane that was donated by Dick's Sporting Goods. They also made arrangements to drive us directly to the hospital.

We arrived at the hospital by 8 a.m. The hospital's Recovery Team left to harvest the organs in Iowa at about 9:30. I waited probably another 6 or 8 hours after that for the surgery to begin. I can't remember. Things get really foggy at that point.

I remember waiting in a pre-op surgery room, unsure of whether or not the transplant would be a "go". Never really knowing for sure. I knew at any time it could all be undone and I could be sent home to wait…again.

We waited as each family member arrived, and the mood was pretty happy and silly for the most part. (Or maybe it was just me, and they were just smiling and nodding at me to placate me as people do when they are around someone who has lost their mind.) At other times, there was just quiet—a grave reminder that for all our excitement, somewhere in Iowa there was a family suffering tremendously at that very moment. Our hearts and prayers went out to them.

Anyway, as I remember it, I was busy chatting away, calling friends and talking with my husband and family, who were all turning darker shades of gray by the time I was taken to surgery. Which was fine, because I needed time, you know, to shave my arms and do other REALLY important things that you do before a heart-lung transplant. And yes, I really did shave my arms. By this time, I had logged enough hours "in house" to know that it is in my best interest to shave. All that hospital tape can be very, very painful.

Funny how I can't remember a thing. But I do remember praying with my mom.

Then, the line between dreams, reality, and hallucinations becomes blurred. I didn't speak, walk, eat, or drink again for another month; and it was longer than that still before I could trust any of my cognitions again. I am not kidding. We are talking months.

-- Liz

<u>*July 13, 2004*</u>
My next "memories" are part dream, part hallucination…

I dreamt (for lack of a better word for it) that I received my organs from an older woman, and that this woman herself was waiting for an organ transplant and had died waiting for the transplant. (My ever-present guilt.) I was with this woman's family in a some type of waiting room, watching their disbelief as they came to terms with their grief, because their family member wasn't supposed to die in this manner; she was supposed to be the recipient of an organ transplant, not the donor.

But my body was not cooperating with the transplant, and soon the doctors realized that her organs were not doing the trick; something was wrong, and I was told they were going to transplant me again.

Next thing I knew, I had been transplanted again; this time with the organs of a 7-year-old girl. I could see her face; it was like a school picture, she had her baseball hat on. I then met her family, who came into the OR and I cried with them; thanking them for the gift they had given me.

The reality during this time was that I WAS transplanted—but only once. But there were serious problems—very serious problems that started midway through my surgery, of which I was unconscious and knew nothing about. But apparently on some level, obviously I did.

The bleeding in my heart refused to stop. I got as close to death as I ever would on this journey. The morning after my surgery, my family was called once again at 5 am, for a second surgery, to stop the bleeding in my heart. The transplant surgeon was clear with them; he hadn't seen many recover from this situation. He also pointed out that they had left me on the heart-lung machine (ECMO) longer than they wanted to, which led to the worry of the possibility of brain damage or a stroke. They had to leave my surgical site open for days, wrapped in some type of medical plastic saran wrap after the surgery, which gave them easy access while they tried to stop the bleeding. A week actually…an entire week.

Let me explain: My incision goes from one armpit, under my breasts, to the other armpit. It is called a clamshell incision, if that gives you any indication of what I looked like. My husband said it was the strangest thing to see—the sheet that covered me moved with my heartbeat and the movement of my lungs.

During this time I also had dreams /hallucinations, ones where I would "leave" the hospital, and go convalesce in other people's homes—my friends' houses specifically. I believed that at night I went to their houses to rest and get care. I distinctly remember my friend PJ telling me she was happy to care for me in her basement, but that it was "time for me to go back to the hospital and get the care I needed". (Incidentally, I really do believe I was visiting with my friends on another psychic level during that time. I needed their support and apparently I was willing to have an out-of-body experience in order to have the support and love I needed.)

When I was brought out of my medically induced coma, I don't remember being in physical pain, but I did suffer tremendously in other ways.

I had a very rough time when I became conscious. Sometimes I was belligerent. I pulled out tubes from myself—fairly regularly—until they tied me down to the bed. If I didn't like what I was being told, I would curse people out and tell them to leave the room. "Get out!", I would mouth, hiss and point. And since I couldn't *speak (because I had a tracheotomy) for the most part, I just gave people the finger instead.*

I would kick the nurses, my husband, and even mother out, depending on my mood.

My hallucinations where having their way with me, and I couldn't speak to share them with anyone. I believed that Scott had lost his job. So I couldn't understand why he wasn't with me 24/7. When I finally got around to asking where he was, they told me he was working. I didn't understand. How could he be working, if he lost his job? So, I then concluded that he must be having an affair. If he wasn't with me, he was with someone else. I was really busy giving him the finger then.

Next I decided that the Department of Social Services was investigating me for child neglect. Because I was unable to take adequate care of my children, I thought I was being investigated. I thought that the psychiatrist, who was assessing and treating my medically-induced psychosis, was, in my mind, the Department of Social Services worker, and for the life of me I couldn't understand why he was just asking ME questions and not my husband. I couldn't understand why Scott was letting me face this man alone. I felt betrayed and abandoned by my husband. I didn't understand, and I couldn't. Even when I was told repeatedly who he was and why he was there, I didn't understand why he was asking me all those very personal questions that had nothing to do with childrearing. Mostly, he asked me where I was and I knew where I was. The hospital, I would him tell over and over, emphatically. But I had difficulty deciding where the hospital was. Every day, they would ask. I would tell them I was at the University of Pittsburgh Medical Center. Then they would ask me where it was located—and sure, that sounds like a no-brainer—to which I would reply, "Binghamton, New York".

You see, for some reason or another, I had decided that I was at UPMC, but in a small part of the hospital that was located in upstate Binghamton, New York. (No such thing exists.) I had decided that each day, this "ward" of the hospital physically flew like a mobile hospital back and forth from Pittsburgh to Binghamton.

When my husband would tell me he had to go home, I couldn't understand why he couldn't just fly with us back in the "mobile" hospital. I couldn't understand why he would want to drive the 6 hours, when the hospital flight took less than an hour…my mind just could not get around this.

*I learned a very simple but valuable lesson about hallucinations: **Don't argue with a crazy person.***

It's just not worth it and they don't believe what they are being told anyway. Save your breath. It is much easier on the crazy person—in this case, me—to just agree with them. Take it from me—everyone is much better off.

For instance, I argued incessantly about being taken to the bathroom. I had "created" a bathroom in my mind that existed down and across the hall. I would ask to be taken there, OVER and OVER.

They would insist there was no such bathroom; I would insist that I had been there. Instead of arguing with me, someone should have just agreed, and said, "Yes there is a bathroom over there—but we think it would be much easier if you went here, Liz, in this bed pan." Instead, we would argue (with a lot of pointing and grunting) over the existence of that bathroom—until I shit myself.

Again and again. Very frustrating, as you might imagine.

The other argument I remember having ad nauseum was over my socks.

Like the tubes that I kept pulling out, I didn't like the socks. You know those therapeutic socks they put on you? The ones that inflate periodically to make your blood circulate? Well, those weren't working for me. And while I couldn't reach them with my hands, that didn't stop me from taking them off. I would use my feet and calves to fight them off. I would take them off; and the staff would put them back on.

I was convinced there were snakes in them, dead ones at that. Talk about freaking myself out. I couldn't keep them on. And so it went, I would take them off. I would get yelled at and they would put them back on again. I would end up frustrated and exhausted, like a naughty toddler, when all I really needed was a new fresh pair of socks with no dead reptiles in them. Instead, I would mumble and try to communicate that there was something inside my socks, they would check, and find nothing. Then, to my dismay they'd slam them right back on my feet. How simple it would have been for any one of them to just say, "Here sweetheart—let me get you a new pair."

*As I said: **Just placate the crazy person**. They'll love you for it.*

Next thing I remember is not having anything to eat or drink for a very long time. Specifically, I remember going 21 days without a drink of water. That's pretty specific for a girl who can't remember a whole hell of a lot.

I remember being unable to move, hooked up to every tube and wire in the room. Staring at the staff outside my room (because it's all encased in glass like an aquarium. Well, let's just say "terrarium", due to the lack of water), while they ate and drank. I watched them with envy as they drank their bottled water.

They would give me a swab with some water on it to suck on, but that was about the extent of it. Once, I bit the swab in half and closed my mouth, refusing to give it back in an act of thirst-fueled defiance. My mother panicked thinking I was going to choke on it, and called the nurses so they could pry my mouth open and grab for it. Again, I was behaving like a naughty toddler. But all I wanted was a drink of water, and to me it seemed like such a simple request. My fantasies consisted of pushing a nurse down in the hallway, grabbing her cold, shiny bottle of Aquafina and making a run for it.

I was desperate for communication, but could not speak because of my tracheotomy. They gave me paper and a pen to write with, but I couldn't, because my hands trembled so badly from the meds that I could barely hold the pen. They wrote things for me so I could point and grunt, but I could not see--my eyesight was blurred by the many drugs. And so I suffered inside my head. Alone.

Lastly, I remember the one visit my children made to me while I was in the ICU. It was all I could handle.

Ironically enough, only Emma, the youngest person in my life, at 7 years old, was able to lip-read, understand, and translate to others what I had been trying to say. And while I had gone off the deep end temporarily, I still knew enough to keep toilets, dead snakes, and Department of Social Services out of the conversation with my daughter. She painted my toenails red during their visit. That I can remember.

Scott blew up a giant picture of my daughters and put it up in my room. It was much easier to deal with the picture version of my girls, and it provided me with the silent but effective motivation for every single waking moment.

And so went the first 5 or 6 weeks of my hospital stay.

-- Liz

> *"People usually consider walking on water or in thin air a miracle.*
> *But I think the real miracle is not to walk either on water or in thin*
> *air, but to walk on earth. Every day we are engaged in a miracle which*
> *we don't even recognize: a blue sky, white clouds, green leaves, the*
> *black, curious eyes of a child -- our own two eyes. All is a miracle."*
>
> *-- THICH NHAT HANH*

We interrupt this traumatic experience to bring some very joyful news:

Today is my new birthday, the anniversary of my transplant!!!

It is either my first birthday, or my 49th (my donor was 48), depending on your point of view.

This is a very exciting day, and ironically I spent the day in Pittsburgh in a hospital bed (just like last year), undergoing tests for my one-year evaluation.

I was done by 1 p.m., and I was in the car, nauseous and vomiting soon thereafter.

No one can ever say I don't know how to party.

All kidding aside, the throwing up was short-lived, and soon my buddy Diane and I were celebrating by having some Chinese food off the interstate. A great way to spend the day.

I feel so lucky and blessed...everyone should be so lucky.

Have a transplant, I highly recommend it. (I never thought I say that, but I mean it.)

You will never look at life the same.

-- Liz

August 2004

<u>*August 2, 2004*</u>
The luxury of being consistently crazy began to fade sometime during the first week of September, and I was finally moved from CTICU (Cardiothoracic Intensive Care Unit) up to a transplant floor. Some things were easier and some were harder. I was not as medicated, which meant I was slightly more coherent---which also meant I now understood the mess I was in. The anger and confusion of being entirely over-medicated had turned to fear. I was scared. I knew I was in rough shape, and in danger of dying; I knew it could happen at any turn. I cried.

    I cried not out of sadness, but rather fear. Fear that I could no longer hold on. Fear that I would not have the strength to keep trying. A fear that I might give up, that I could give up. That fear quickly morphed into grief--grief for myself, as I was all too painfully aware that I was dying. Only my parents saw my tears run down my face, which unraveled them in a way that kept me from doing it too often. Instead, I tried to sleep every chance they would give me (which is not much if you have ever spent any length of time in a hospital bed).

    I relished any moment, conscious or unconscious, where I was not aware of my reality.

    Eating was nothing more than a horrific chore. I could barely chew and swallow without choking or throwing it up. I would eat tiny deliberate bites of mostly soft things like applesauce, yogurt, noodles, and mashed-up something or other, and still had no luck. The doctors would stand in a pack in my room trying to decide how they could help me regain some eating skills while I vomited up the little I ate in front of them. I was losing weight, and the doctors were concerned. Finally, I pulled out my feeding tube (by accident? on purpose?), and refused/ begged to not have it replaced.

    They threatened to put the feeding tube back only at night, reasoning that I could continue to practice eating on my own during the day. I argued that if they fed me all night, I would never be hungry and motivated to eat during the day. They held off on replacing the feeding tube. They tested everything to make sure my esophagus was in working order, and found nothing they could fix. They made my mother start keep track of every sip and bite I took. My mom would write *"one-half cup of soup", or,"2 bites of a banana". I would argue with her and the nurses that it was **three-quarters** cup soup and at least **half** of the banana-- that was how tragically mundane my existence had become. Scott would bring in all kinds of yummy treats to entice me and mostly I would glaze over, not caring about what would, on a normal day, leave me salivating, overjoyed, and doing the happy-food dance.*

Eating a minuscule meal could take anywhere from 30 minutes to an hour; and then I would have to swallow pills which could easily take another 45 minutes.

Finally it was time to go sit in the chair, which sounds like a respite to most of us, but was, in reality, my activity for the morning. Getting there left me out of breath; and then sitting there, holding myself up, was like strenuous exercise.

Finally, I would get back into bed only to have lunch delivered, and start all over again.

Physically, much more was expected of me. I was sitting in a chair in the mornings and in the afternoon. Physical therapists would help me learn and relearn simple things that most of us take for granted--like how to get up out of the bed, how to shift from bed to chair, how to stand, etc. Then, 2 of them would hold me, arm-in-arm, and walk 10- or 20 feet down the hallway and back. There are no words to describe how excruciating and exhausting these activities were.

I was still using a bedpan, and they began encouraging me to use a commode, which might as well have been an Olympic event in terms of magnitude of event.

In between, I slept. Happily.

I was still having hallucinations; only they were milder, less invasive and less violent. More importantly, I was open to believing that the things I was hallucinating were not, in fact, true. A huge step in recovering.

I whispered conspiratorially to my mother, "This hospital is really very nice except for the rats."—and the disappointed look on her face let me know that I had it all wrong.

"There are no rats here, Liz."

It was hard for her to think I was still in that crazy place. Fortunately, I wasn't there all the time. I just went for small visits. But you never knew when visiting hours were.

Other family members came for a few days at a time to give my mother a much-needed break from my lunacy. My father, father-in-law, sister-in-law, and sister came for stints, and mostly I just remember hating having to retrain each person in the skills it took to take care of me.

During my stay on the seventh floor, I had a few milestones that I remember in full detail. The first exciting event was that I had my hair washed. The nurse scootched me up to the top of the bed, and while I was lying down, she washed my hair; I remember being so impressed with her technique.

The next milestone came when my sister-in-law Bridget came to visit. Two months into my hospitalization, I took a shower. This I was excited for in theory, but the reality was not easy or pleasant.

It was a large walk in shower with a bar to hold on to and a chair to sit in. The first problem we encountered was the steam. I could barely breathe with the steam, which meant we had to cool down the water to lessen the steam--which in turn left me literally convulsing with chills from the cooler water. Finally, we found that if we turned up the water temperature and left the door open for the steam to escape, I didn't tremble as much. I was unable to stand, so I sat in the chair while my sister-in-law scrubbed and cleaned my 36-year-old frail little old lady body. Finally, it came time for me to stand and to try to wash my own "private" area (and I use that term loosely because there is nothing private about being naked and frail in the shower while someone else does everything for you).

So I stood and held on to the shower bar for dear life. **Kinda like riding the 7 train, I thought.**

As I said--in the end, there was nothing even remotely pleasant about this experience except for the fact that it left me clean and with the knowledge that I could do it again when I needed to.

After some time passed, these showers, to my complete surprise, did become slightly more manageable; and over time my mom and I had them down to a quick and painful half-hour activity.

On the medical front during this time, I was struggling with some problems with a Strep B virus, and Level 2 rejection issues. There was some evidence of pulmonary necrosis (tissue death in the lungs), and some cell/tissue damage within the lungs—and both the pathologists and the transplant doctors were not exactly sure why.

Also at some point, the doctors installed a vena cava filter. I didn't even know it was there until months after my surgery. The vena cava is one of the main veins in the body, and it carries oxygen-depleted blood to the right side of the heart. If a clot breaks free from my lower body, it could pass via the blood through the heart, and over to the lungs—very bad news. It's the job of the filter in my vena cava to catch any clots and keep them from traveling to my lungs. But because of my abdominal hematoma a couple of weeks back, they were interested in me not "springing another leak".

Lastly, they downsized my tracheostomy tube from a size 6 to size 4, which was a welcome step in the direction of being rid of that damn thing once and for all. I had also gotten rid of the face mask, and graduated to just a nasal cannula for oxygen delivery to help with my breathing. Who knew that breathing could be so hard and require practice, diligence and such hard work? Basically, if having pulmonary hypertension was like breathing through a straw- then moving from a face mask to a cannula was like breathing through a coffee stirrer. Pure torture. Respiratory therapists had become the enemy.

And so, slowly the shift began for me physically, but the mental shift would take many more months. I could not find any joy. I was in dark emotional void. Only now in retrospect do I understand the experience as Post-traumatic Stress Disorder (PTSD). The experience in the hospital completely traumatized me, and I was left in big black hole looking out at the rest of the world.

People would be overjoyed and thrilled to call me, see me—but I could not muster up even an ounce of anything in return. I felt extremely bad for my husband and children who I knew deserved more than a blank-faced wife and mother.
    -- Liz

August 10, 2004
This past weekend I had the joy and pleasure of meeting my transplant friend Allison and her family. We met in Vermont and spent the weekend playing and getting to know each other. What a wondrous time it was. Close friends of ours had us all over to their home, and there we played, did art projects with the kids, and ate our way through the weekend.

What a long, strange trip…to meet my now-longtime cyber friend in the real world.

If you have ever thought that your life was boring, that every day was blasé, routine, or not exciting enough, think just for a moment about what it would be like if you couldn't walk, breathe, or for that matter even talk. Allison and I are all too familiar with it.

Every day, in many ways, we are blessed. It's our job to realize that the blessings are sitting there in a big huge pile, just waiting to be acknowledged, received, and accepted.

It is our job to notice those blessings, to not overlook or take them for granted; to live with them and treasure them, and then to share them--so that others can know that they too, are blessed.

-- Liz

My 37th birthday at the family house in Pittsburgh.

Also my birthday with my Dad and the girls.

More birthday!

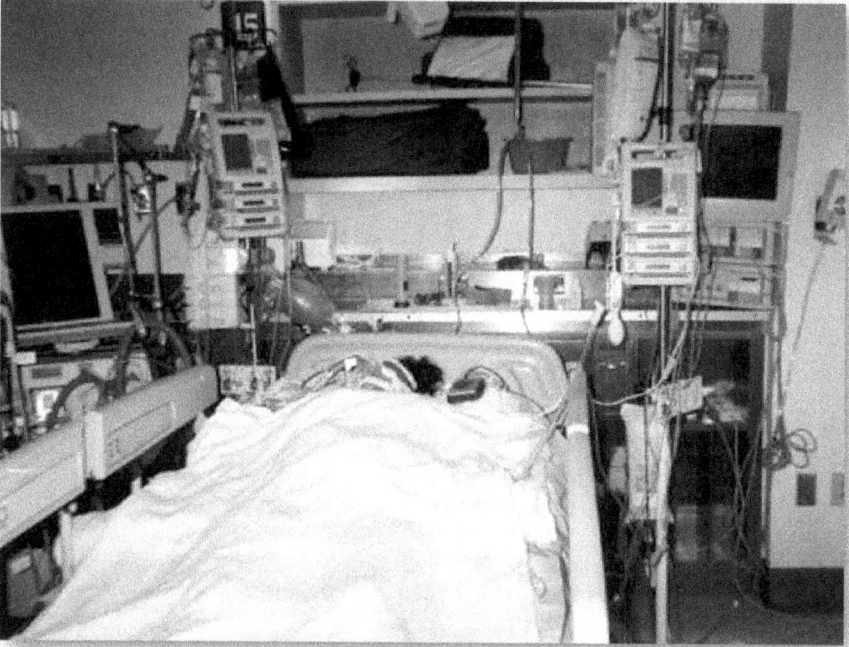

Post-transplant, these are not pretty.

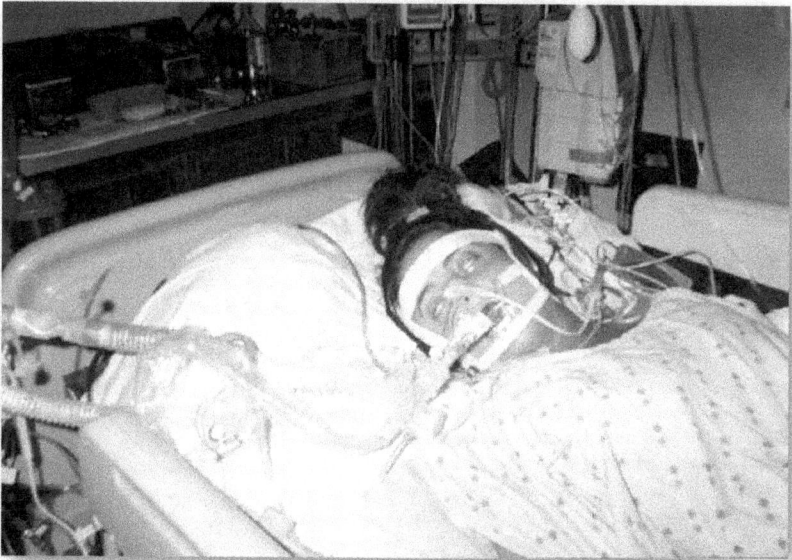

Like I said, not pretty.

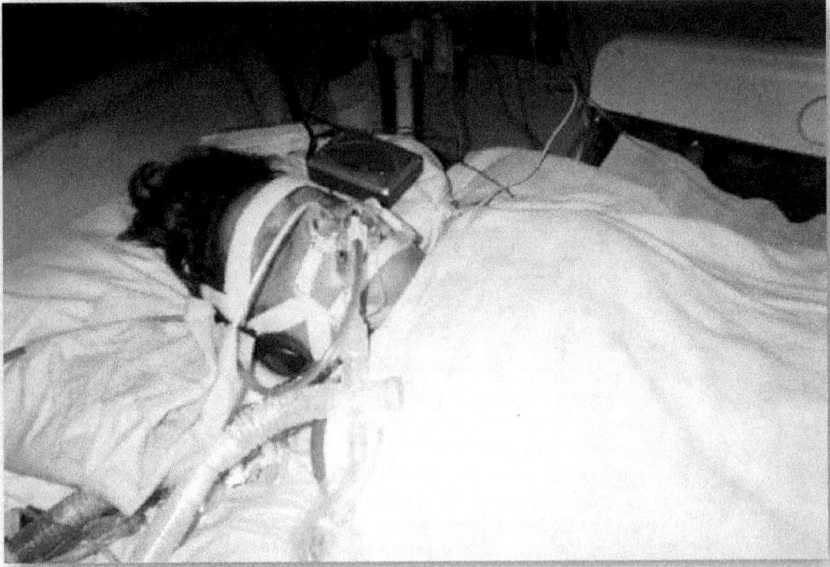

Me plugged in to everything including my old school Walkman.

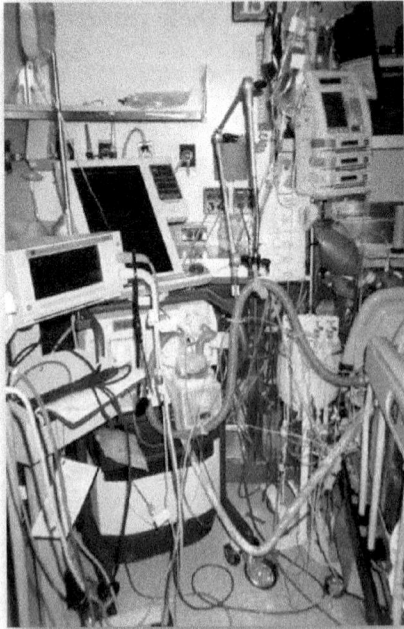

Enough wires and tubes?

August 17, 2004

I finally wrote my donor family a letter of thanks; it has taken me all this time to finally get around to it.

Not because I am "so busy" or anything like that, but rather because initially, I was not ready emotionally…and then more recently, I could never find the adequate words to express myself. This is not a task for a Hallmark thank-you card.

How do you thank someone who had a family member die so that you could live? Adequately? It's a near impossible task for mere words to do.

Very difficult. But necessary, I decided. After talking with some other organ recipients, I finally got up the "nerve"--for a lack of a better word--and wrote.

The one key piece of advice that I received was, Don't worry if you don't say everything you want; you can always write again.

Sounds simple doesn't it? But it really released me from the pressure of having to say it all.

Once I realized that this letter didn't have to be the be-all and end-all, I then felt more comfortable writing the letter. It is still 4 pages long. So after many months of putting it off…I did it.

It is confidential, as I don't know who this family is and they don't know who I am. The letter goes to CORE, an agency that acts as the intermediary, and sends the letters along to the family, who, if they wish, can write a letter back to me.

I may hear back from them…and I may never hear another word.

My hope is that they write back, as I would like to learn more about my donor. What an amazing gift to give life to a complete stranger.

It still blows me away, every day.

-- Liz

August 28, 2004

ARGGHH. Back to my transplant…

After another 4 weeks or so, the time came for me to be moved to inpatient rehabilitation. All it meant to me at the time was that I would now be able to wear some regular clothes and ditch the hospital gowns. What I didn't realize in my excitement was that it took effort and strength to change into and out of clothes every day, twice a day.

This time I not only changed rooms, but hospitals as well. Every day was comprised of two 45-minute periods of physical therapy, two 45-minute periods of occupational therapy, and one 45-minute period of "recreational" therapy (and I use that word lightly; it's all tiring).

I was on my own much more often now. The nurses only came in sporadically to check my vitals. I took this as a sign that they felt confident in me. Me? -- not so much.

I got up one of my first mornings in rehab, and stood looking at the locker/ shelf where my clothes and sneakers were that I had to change in to. I contemplated my method of attack. When I reached down to get the sneakers (which were on a shelf maybe 18 inches up off the floor), I lost my balance and literally tipped over backwards; I was still connected to an IV pole at the time, and had the misfortune of smashing my head into the bottom of the metal pole.

I lay splayed out on the ground, half under the bed. I assessed the pain and tried to figure out how in the hell I landed like this--and more importantly, how to get out. I couldn't roll over to my knees, I didn't have the strength.

I tried to "yell" for help. But really the best I was mustering voice-wise was a loud whisper. But I still tried yelling—"I need help, please"--over and over until I was crying in frustration. No one was coming to check on me. I was starting to panic, and the call bell was up on top of the bed. I was under it.

I tried laying there patiently, thinking someone would come check on me.

No one did. Finally, I tried wiggling on the floor; I could see the wire for the call bell dangling at the other end of the bed. I used my foot to pull the call bell down to the ground. I was never so happy to push that little red button.

At first when the nurse came in the room, she couldn't even find me. When she found me she was more than a little puzzled as to how I got there. I and I was too tired to explain my last half-hour journey to her, so all is I said was, "I was just trying to put my shoes on." She laced them up for me sympathetically in all of about 15 seconds. Bitch. My life, not the nurse.

It was the beginning of October when I finally moved to the family house, the last stop before I could go home. While I was excited to leave the hospital, the novelty of the family house wore out quickly. I was excited to sleep in a nice bed, to have my girls visit for extended periods of time, and eat what I wanted when I wanted. But that was only in theory.

My reality was much harder to bear. I needed to get dressed every day, go down to the kitchen to eat (a 45-minute endeavor), come back up and take pills--another 45-minute chore if I didn't choke or throw them back up and have to start all over again. I was taking well over 20 medicines a day at that point. Rest and start all over again. In between, the physical therapist would come every other day and encourage me to walk, or climb stairs. There were about 6-8 steps that I practiced on in the stairwell, it was pure torture and I came to really hate the sight of that stairwell.

I would also go to the clinic at the hospital where they would monitor my progress. This is where my mother would rat me out: "She is not eating enough, she spends too much time in bed, she doesn't want to do anything." I would get angry with her for telling the doctors these things, but she was right. I didn't want to eat, get up or do anything--it was all too much and too overwhelming for me. It was official: I was despondent.

Worse, I was losing weight. A significant sign that all was not OK in my world, I was readmitted for another week while they tried to figure out if there was some concrete reason for my inability to eat. They didn't find anything, so back to the family house I went.

I went through an array of caregivers at this point: my mother, my father, my husband, my father-in-law, my brother, my sister, my friends. Everyone came to take a turn, again.

Now it was November, and the doctors where thinking that perhaps after Christmas I could go home. My heart and spirits sank to new low levels. I knew I had to get out of there. Instinctively I knew the only road out of the mess I was in was to go home. I knew that at home, I would put my children's needs before my own, that they would motivate me in ways I was not able to, sitting there in the family house.

My family already had come to terms with me not coming home until after the holidays, but I hadn't. At my next clinic visit, I spoke with my doctors. I wanted to know what it would take for them to let me go home. They were specific: they wanted me to show weight gain instead of weight loss at my next clinic visit.

My girlfriends Beth and Diane, knowing how desperate I was, came to visit me in Pittsburgh that next weekend. They helped lift my spirits, and they force fed me the entire weekend. They even had to force feed me a cannoli.(there's a couple words I have never used in a sentence together) The next clinic appointment came, and when I weighed in 2 pounds heavier, I knew I was free.

I went back to the family house, called my disbelieving husband and told him, "Come pick me up; I am spending Thanksgiving at home."

And I did.

-- Liz

> *The standard of success in life isn't the things. It isn't the money or the stuff -- it is absolutely the amount of joy you feel.*
> *--- ABRAHAM HICKS*

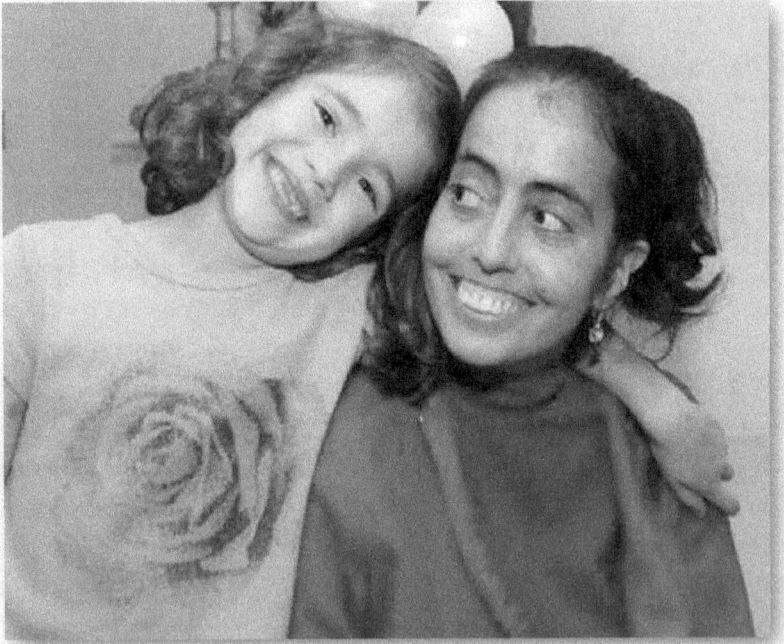

Courtesy of Press and Sun Bulletin

This was the picture on the front page of our newspaper the day I came home. The title of the article was "MOMMY'S HOME!".

2012

～

Nine years have triumphantly passed since my transplant--not without my fair share of physical and emotional bumps in the road, I might add. I have had my fair share of medical "stuff" with my gall bladder being removed, a pacemaker put in for complete heart block (we discovered that after passing out a few times and a few stiches), many a hospitalization, many episodes of infection--Aspergillus and Nocardia, along with a few bouts of Clostridium difficile—and also a couple of episodes of rejection. Yes, the dreaded "chronic rejection". I hate that terminology for sure; and just for the record, I just had the best pulmonary function tests I have had in about 2 years--so poo-poo on you, "chronic rejection". (Maybe I will worry about it if I actually feel badly, but not until then. Right now, I see it as just a poorly-worded diagnosis.)

In the meantime, all the anti-rejection meds are taking their toll on my kidneys. I have Stage 3 kidney disease at this time. It's quite common for people who have been transplanted to develop kidney disease, and ultimately need a kidney transplant. Maybe there will be kidney transplant in my future, and maybe not. Either way, I am ready.

My rheumatologist says that if he didn't know that I have scleroderma, he wouldn't be able to identify it by looking at me, which I think is just fabulous.

All in all, I feel fabulous.

I have been able to see my children grow up into ornery teenagers (lucky me!). All kidding aside, I was able to see my oldest graduate from high school, something that ten years ago I barely had the capacity to dream about, because it seemed such a farfetched fantasy. Last week I moved Luci into her college dorm. I am thinking the word bittersweet was created just for instances just like this...because really, there were no other words to describe the experience.

I volunteer regularly with Center for Donation and Transplant based in Albany, New York, talking about organ donation with any one that will have me--high school students, nursing students, medical students—whoever. When invited, I will come. I also speak with newly hired health care providers, nurses, doctors, residents and interns. I share my experiences with them in hopes of helping them do their job a little bit better, with a little more compassion.

I have also returned to work part time as a social worker in a dialysis facility. I really enjoy working with chronically ill patients.

I have been able to travel quite a bit, mainly to visit my father and my family in Colombia, South America. It has been wonderful in so many ways to reconnect with my family there. My kids have a relationship with their cousins and second cousins that I would have never dreamed possible, and for which I am very thankful and grateful. I have traveled to other cool places as well, mostly with my ever-adventurous mother.

Sadly, there have been some tremendous losses in the past 8 years as well.

My marriage ended--after being together for 23 years and weathering many a crisis, and unfortunately, a few more betrayals (including an affair with a neighbor and family friend who helped our family fundraise close to $30,000.00 for my transplant). When I finally surrendered it wasn't even the betrayals that made me throw in the towel (although that should have been enough) it was the contempt and disrespect in his eyes, and the fact that my children were learning the same contempt and disrespect for me by his example. In the end, we grew to become two different people who wanted different things from life. I sadly mourned the end of my family as I knew it. This was a tragic realization for me to come to terms with, given that it was for my family that I choose to live; but in the end I realized that if I wanted to keep living, it was the choice that had to be made. It was very hard to let go of the family I fought for, for so long and for so hard.

> *"Love never dies a natural death. It dies because we don't know how to*
> *replenish it's source. It dies of blindness and errors and betrayals. It dies*
> *of illness and wounds; it dies of weariness, of witherings, of tarnishings."*
> *-- ANAIS NIN*

My father and my father-in-law both passed away within a couple of years of each other, which was just heartbreaking because I loved them both so much, and they loved me with all their hearts. I spent so many years just assuming that I would be the first to go, that their passing before me was just unfathomable--and so very hard to come to terms with.

Now I take solace in knowing that finally there are people "there" before me; and I look forward to that time when we meet again in the Light.

I am still not scared of dying, only sad to leave the people I love.

Now, believe it or not, I have entered a new chapter of my life. It just me and Emma at home now (and 2 dogs and 2 cats). And yes I am dating. Me dating? Who can believe that a person such as me, with so much history of illness, despair, and injuries, both emotional and physical, could be dating? Certainly not me. But I am. I have even been blessed enough to find love--in a relationship with a man who is tender, loving, smart, respectful, and ever-thoughtful.

So life moves on; or as my 93-year-old Tia Rosita in Colombia says, p'alante.

Ironically enough, my transplant soul sister, Allison, is weathering the exact same changes as I, and we continue to marvel at our parallel lives. But at any rate, as my life continues to change as I grow older, I continue to change and accept the changes gratefully and gracefully. And after all these years my plan is still simple: To live my life fabulously, and lovingly.

Liz DeVivo

"Happy is the heart that still feels pain
Darkness drains and light will come again
Swing open your chest and let it in
Just let the love, love, love begin
Everybody, everybody wants to love
Everybody, everybody wants to be loved"
-- INGRID MICHAELSON

More lessons for health care professionals

⟿

1. You have heard this a million times before in school, but it's so important I am going to say it again: *Listen*.

W hether it's for 4 minutes that you are with me, the patient, or 40 minutes, it doesn't matter. What matters is that you are fully present with me, the patient, when you are with me. I know it's easier said than done, because you are thinking of the 8 things that need to be done after meeting with me, and the 8 things you did before meeting with me. (And your stomach is growling!) It doesn't matter how long you meet with me, just listen. Patients hold many clues to their illness and sometimes even the answer! This is a talent or skill that takes mindful practice, something you will have to train yourself to do.

Make a commitment to yourself right now, that you will train yourself to do this and have it become part of your regular practice.

2. Sit down with me, face to face please. Look up from your computer!

Don't stand above me like a boss or parent giving me directions. Consider me a partner in my health, I mean, really--we both want the same thing, right? For me to get better?

If you walk into my hospital room, please introduce yourself, don't just dive into my plan of care without identifying yourself and your specialty. Sometimes I have multiple providers, each of course, with their own agenda and plan.

3. Don't interrupt me; let me finish my thought.

Again, it's part of that "clue and answer" thing--there may be some useful information that may help with a diagnosis.

4. Ask questions not only about my illness, but about my experience with illness.

Someone who has seen the same problem before, say for the last 10 years might have some previous information that might be helpful with treatment or diagnosis vs. someone who has never seen the problem before. For example, if a patient says, "You can't put a PICC line in my right arm, as it has had several lines before, and even interventional radiologists prefer my left arm", vs. another patient who says, "Put in my right arm because I like to stick the left one out the window when I drive." Which of course is not critical information, unless perhaps they drive for a living, and then it IS critical information.

5. The simple question 'What has helped you in the past?" is great for more info and clues on solving the mystery (think of yourself as the great inspector in a classic mystery novel).

If I tell you something along the lines of, "Well, it doesn't hurt or bother me as much when I sleep on my left side", then guess what? That's another clue--like perhaps it's my heart.

Conversely, if you ask a patient, "What has helped you in the past?"— and they answer, "Drinking a 12-pack of beer helps."--well you know you have another issue to address now, and you don't have to wonder why your 30-year-old patient's liver is shot.

I think you get my point.

6. Don't disregard our knowledge of ourselves.

While I know patients (including myself) all think that we can diagnose ourselves, (with the help of the internet, *of course*). Don't blow us off...

instead; ask us WHY we think this? Again you may find out something crucial like "oh because my mom had it."

These same questions may get you some very real individual answers for what is helpful. If a patient tells you yoga helps them feel better, praying the rosary daily, or rubbing their elbows in paprika every night before bed makes the pain go away, don't discount this. It may not exist in the current literature, and perhaps never will. Humbly accept that it may not be traditional medicine that brings your patient pain relief or healing. If a patient believes something is helping them, you need to believe them, regardless of whether or not you believe it, and especially if it can't be proven. Many roads lead to Rome. (As long as they are not hurting themselves of course!)

7. Please consider the best interest of the patient, don't get territorial on me.

Do what's best for me, if you think I would be better served by a different specialist or in a different hospital, then tell me. Protect *me*--not your wallet, your research, business, or hospital.

8. Let's talk about medications for a minute.

I know you want to help me and I know I want to get better. Please give the medications that will help me get there. And then when I am better, please revisit these medications regularly to ensure that I still need them. You guys are great at giving meds out and lousy at taking them away! I realize there are meds (in particular for me as a transplant patient) that I will always need to take. But when other issues pop up, don't be so quick to prescribe another pill.

As an example: When the immunosuppressants I take gave me headaches, I was given something for headaches that made it harder for me to sleep; then I was given something for sleep that made me itchy, and then I was given something else for the itch...you get the picture now? I would rather deal with the headaches as they come, than the mountain of pills and side effects (never mind the money spent for all those prescriptions). As a result, I say "no" to pills that I don't feel were necessary, much to the frustration of my provider. I have learned over time that the less meds there are in my body at any point, the better I feel. I don't have a problem lying in a dark room for a couple hours when a headache arrives. It's a tradeoff and choice that I make and I hope you can respect me for.

9. Talk and coordinate my care with my other providers.

I realize this is extremely difficult considering the time constraints that exist in your daily schedule. However you must realize some patients require more of your resources and some less. Don't think of this as "not fair", because when everyone gets what he or she needs, that is in fact "fair". Along the same lines, don't be afraid that if you do something above and beyond for a patient, that you will have to do it for everyone; it just doesn't happen that way. Again, "fair" is when everyone gets what they need.

10. PLEASE, PLEASE, PLEASE reconsider the use of the terms "Non-compliant" or "Difficult".

Patients who are not following your care plan or not taking the meds you prescribed are not doing it because they are stubborn or bad. They are not "out to get you", and they are not trying to screw you over. In fact it (usually) has nothing to do with you at all. It's about us. Ask us, "Why aren't you taking the medication?" Or better yet, "What do you think can help you take this medication/ treatment?"

You might be surprised at the answer. It could be as simple as, "The medicine is unaffordable." Or perhaps it gives the person a side effect that is either more scary or worse than the symptom you are treating. I have had this happen-- where a medication I was prescribed gave me headaches for up to 8 hours the next day. Now why in the world would I willingly take that?

When I refused a feeding tube, it wasn't because I was "non-compliant" (although there is nothing more fearful for a potential transplant patient to be labeled), it was because I couldn't stomach the idea of parenting with more tubes and lines coming out of me. I already had a double-lumen catheter hooked up to two continuous IV pumps hanging on my body. You try bending over and zippering a jacket or giving a 5-year-old a bath with all that sticking out of you. I made a choice. I would rather force feed myself than deal with another tube. I also bargained with my doctor that within a certain time frame, if things did not change, I would reconsider the feeding tube. The doctor was agreeable to this. It's ok to make a deal, and negotiate "terms". It doesn't mean you have lost, if patients disagree with you, and it certainly doesn't hurt your authority.

ASK. Only then can you help problem solve or troubleshoot. Maybe another medication, a patient assistance program, or some other creative idea can help. Enlisting help from extended family is also a great way to help patients get on board. I think my point is clear. Be willing and flexible to do what's best for each patient. Again, many roads lead to Rome.

11. This piece of advice might raise some hackles, but I will try to be gentle. Remember unless you are a member of the transplant community, or you just happen to know all the exclusion criteria for all the transplant centers in the U.S, you have very little reason to tell people they are not candidates for a transplant.

I not only say this from first-hand experience (being told "no" at Mount Sinai in New York City, and then "yes" at Pittsburgh), but from countless other transplant recipients or would-be recipients telling me similar stories.

A person who was told she was not a candidate for a liver transplant by her primary doctor was encouraged by her family to go for a transplant evaluation. She didn't go because she felt badly "going behind her primary doctor's back". Years later, she finally got up the courage, and was listed at a center, only to die waiting. She could have, and should have, been listed sooner. Another woman I know was given a liver even though she had just finished treatment for ovarian cancer within the past 6 months (generally, you have to be cancer-free for 2 years). And lastly, what may be a rule-out today may be treatable or curable tomorrow. HIV was a rule-out for kidney transplants only a few years ago, and that no longer holds true. I like to tell the patients I work with 'don't rule yourself out' I tell you now too. Unless you are a member of the transplant community, or you work with a population that is regularly being transplanted like a nephrologist at a dialysis center, you have very little reason to tell people they are not candidates for a transplant. (My apologies to the transplant centers who would like fewer referrals)

12. Most importantly, and I said it before and I will say it again: Don't take away our hope.

It protects our greatest weapon against illness, *our mind*. (And I hate the word "weapon", because I hate all metaphors that refer to illness as the enemy.) I prefer to say that hope is our greatest ally in healing our bodies. And no, it's not just semantics. It's time to consider the placebo effect as a positive outcome.

I was diagnosed with a simple, "I am sorry". I was furious. There were many other alternate wording options that could have been more useful.

Later when talking about this subject with resident doctors in a classroom setting, they would ask me, "Well, then how would you have preferred that conversation to have gone?"

I would have preferred, "I don't know much about the disease myself but there are specific pulmonary hypertension specialists who deal with illness exclusively that can help you better understand what you're facing."

Or perhaps, suggesting a particular hospital that is doing extensive research on pulmonary hypertension.

Or maybe finding an organization, support group or online resource (of which there were many, I would soon learn) to help a person. There were many options that would not cut off hope at the kneecaps.

Or from a group of medical students, the question would arise: "Isn't it sometimes worse to give patients a sense of false hope?" This is a GREAT question, except for the fact that science, technology, and medicine change so rapidly that what may hold true today maybe completely wrong and out-dated 5, or even 2 years from now. And research quickly becomes outdated, often before it is even published. The changes I have seen in the treatment in pulmonary hypertension alone in the last 10 years are astounding. The quicker you humbly admit to yourself that you don't know everything, the better a doctor you will be.

Hope can never be bad thing.

> *"All these psychics and these doctors,*
> *They're all right and they're all wrong,*
> *It's like trying to make out every word,*
> *When they should simply hum along,*
> *It's not some message written in the dark,*
> *Or some truth that no one's seen,*
> *It's a little bit of everything…."*
> -- DAWES

Acknowledgements

I would like to acknowledge many people for helping me through this endeavor. Just going down the list has me in tears. First, my lovely girls - Luci and Emma who probably still to this day will never grasp the effect their mere existence had on my survival I have a sneaking suspicion that you will both grow up to be strong resilient women. My amazing Mami, Lucia DeVivo who has always encouraged and cheered me on, first through my illness, then later to finish this project. My brother and sister, Joe DeVivo and Janet Crimmins, my nieces, nephews and in-laws. Of course, my beautiful and wonderful beau Scott MacGregor (yes another, different Scott) whose love has helped make me happy, healthy and whole again.

To my lovely fathers, which I was so lucky to have two of! My own father Jose DeVivo and Fred Searles, who now are in charge of keeping me out of trouble from up above. Fred, I don't think it's possible for me to give you anymore gray hairs, which is a relief I am sure - for both of us. And my Papi, who I speak to all the time, just no longer by phone. I miss him terribly every day.

To the lovely Searles family, who continue to show me that love does not simply go away or disappear because of divorce.

I would like to thank my amazing doctors, in Vestal, NY, Doctor Chisdak, my pulmonologist for the last 13 years, who so graciously accepts the task of also acting as my primary doctor, no easy task, and his wonderful staff there. In New York City, Doctor Harry Spiera, my rheumatologist who kept me on task to survive when my will faltered, and it did.

My wonderful team in Pittsburgh, PA at University of Pittsburgh Medical Center of doctors, nurses, transplant coordinators and all the other wonderful staff over the past decade, in particular, Doctor Michael Mathier, my heart failure specialist, who once said what he thought was the most innocuous sentence ever I am sure, when he said, 'Liz, I will see you in 20 years.' (I am planning on it!) My amazing and skillful surgeon Doctor Kenneth McCurry (who is now at Cleveland Clinic) and my hero Doctor Maria Crespo, who started her fellowship when I had my transplant and has followed and put up with me ever since!

A very big thanks to Dicks Sporting Goods for supplying my angel flight on my very important day.

All the amazing angels who read my blog when it was happening, and kept me in their prayers and kept in touch with me and helped me to hold on, when I didn't think it was possible.

I would also like to thank all the people that came out of my past, to help our family with fundraising. All my friends from "The Hood", in Woodside, Queens. All the girls, from my all girl high school, St Agnes or "Faggie Aggie's" as we so politically incorrectly call ourselves. My wonderful caring family in Barranquilla, Colombia. All the folks who reached out and helped from The First All Children's Theatre, In particular the Swartz family, Meridee Stein and Michael Feigin who over the years, either encouraged me to keep writing, helped to fundraise, or pushed me to get involved with the government regarding Medicare rulings and transplants.

Thanks to the Scleroderma Foundation and Pulmonary Hypertension Association for all the education, outreach and support over the years.

Here at home I have so many folks to be thankful for. All the people that came out to help our family with fundraising, cooking, cleaning and car pools. My wonderful and supportive friends and neighbors in the 'Greater Binghamton Area', he he I giggle as I write it, but it really is The GREATER Binghamton area, for many reasons. While I can't stand the cold here, in many ways it's the warmest place I have ever lived. A special thanks to all the teachers, staff, children and parents at the Vestal School District that helped us get through, one day at a time, in particular the Heichemer family who has always been there to help support my family in every way possible.

All the prayer groups and prayer chains who held me up in prayer literally, all over the world.

I am grateful to and for my soul sister Allison Lyne, may both of our journeys continue to be blessed.

A very special thank you to all the wonderful healers who shared their gifts with me, Amadeus, Annette Kozel and Maryanne Harter for helping to heal me for years and years, in many ways medicine cannot.

My lovely pack of girlfriends, especially Beth Harrington, Karla Rizzuto, Nancy Heichemer, Laurie Abess, Jo Ann Sexton, Jodi and Karen Lowry, Bridget Searles, Irene Loverdos, Carey Harben and Letty McGrath, who helped from close and afar ......I don't know what I would do without you. You all pulled me from the dark black abyss of despair on more than one occasion. I am always happy to celebrate living with friends like you!

For all my wonderful friends who took the time to read this book and critique it.

Finally, my beautiful angel donor, who till this day remains anonymous to me, and who I thank on a daily basis for the gift of my second life.

This book was a labor of love and pain, and if it helps even one person find hope and hold on, even for another day, then I have done my job.

Books And Other Resources That Helped Me On My Journey

Anything by the following authors:
Elizabeth Kübler Ross, Wayne Dyer, Rachel Naomi Remen, Deepak Chopra, Gary Zukav, Louise Hay, Doreen Virtue, Caroline Myss, Eckhart Tolle, Don Miguel Ruiz, Bernie Siegal.

You can follow Amadeus on Facebook or Twitter under "Wisdomgate"

Helpful Websites:
www.organdonor.gov –Sign up to become a donor!

www.Unos.org - Transplant data and information.

http://www.lotsahelpinghands.com/ - To organize help and create community

http://www.cdtny.org/ - Center for Donation and Transplant

www.Scleroderma.org - Scleroderma Foundation, information and patient support

http://www.phassociation.org/ - Pulmonary Hypertension Association

http://www.patientslikeme.com/ - Connect with people like you, learn from others and track your health

http://www.volunteerpilots.org/pr.html - Angel Flights for patients in the Mid-Atlantic

www.lizdevivo.com - All about me!!!

About the Author

Liz DeVivo lives in Upstate New York, but was born and raised in Queens. She is a mother, a heart and double lung transplant recipient, a social worker, speaker, therapist and holistic life coach. She holds an MSW from the State University of New York in Albany and a Masters in Social Sciences from Binghamton University. She missed most of her thirties due to illness and now is happily making up for lost time.

www.ingramcontent.com/pod-product-compliance
Lightning Source LLC
LaVergne TN
LVHW052019080426
835513LV00018B/2091